Do we validate for aggravation?

by Cathy Guisewite

Selected Cartoons from
ONLY LOVE CAN BREAK A HEART, BUT A SHOE SALE COMES CLOSE

FAWCETT CREST • NEW YORK

A Fawcett Crest Book
Published by Ballantine Books

Library of Congress Catalog Card Number: 93-90721

ISBN 0-449-22245-4

This edition published by arrangement with Andrews and McMeel, a Universal Press Syndicate Company

This title is comprised of portions of ONLY LOVE CAN BREAK A HEART, BUT A SHOE SALE CAN COME CLOSE.

Printed in Canada

First Ballantine Books Edition: March 1994

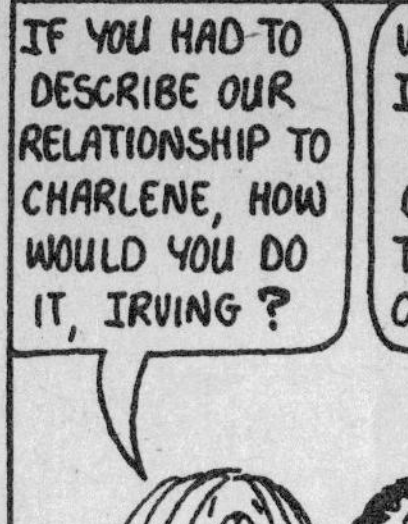
IF YOU HAD TO DESCRIBE OUR RELATIONSHIP TO CHARLENE, HOW WOULD YOU DO IT, IRVING ?

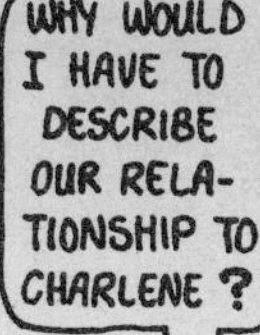
WHY WOULD I HAVE TO DESCRIBE OUR RELA-TIONSHIP TO CHARLENE ?

WELL, SAY YOU FELT YOU HAD TO DEFEND IT.
WHY WOULD I HAVE TO DEFEND IT ?

WELL, SAY YOU WERE ME AND YOU WANTED TO.
WHY WOULD I WANT TO?
WHY WOULDN'T YOU WANT TO ??
WHY WOULD YOU WANT ME TO WANT TO ???

IT'S NONE OF YOUR BUSINESS, CHARLENE ?!
I KNEW IT! THEY'RE IN TROUBLE!

I KNOW IT'S MORE FUN TO SIT HERE. AND TALK ABOUT HOW PERFECT WE ARE, CATHY...

...BUT LOOK AT US! I'VE STARTED TO REALLY LOOK AND I SEE FLAWS...BLEMISHES... I SEE THAT WE'VE BOTH DONE AS MUCH TO SABOTAGE OUR LOVE LIVES AS THE MEN WE...
AACK!! I DON'T WANT TO KNOW!! I DON'T WANT TO LOOK! DON'T MAKE ME LOOK!!

GIRLFRIEND AS MAGNIFIED MAKEUP MIRROR.
I AM NOT LOOKING.

I'LL CALL IRVING AND ASK WHAT HE'S DOING. HE'LL SAY "NOTHING."

I WILL IMMEDIATELY BE OFFENDED THAT HE WAS DOING "NOTHING" AND DIDN'T CALL ME. HE'D OBVIOUSLY RATHER SIT IN A TOTAL, EMPTY, NOTHING VOID THAN BE WITH ME. HAH!

RING RING

HI, CATHY. WHAT ARE YOU DOING?
NOTHING.

DO YOU HAVE ANYTHING ELSE ?
THERE'S $10,000 OF VALENTINE MERCHANDISE OUT HERE, AND YOU HAVE ALREADY FONDLED EVERY PIECE.
VAL

WE ONLY HAVE THREE DAYS TO MAKE UP FOR OUR DISASTROUS CHRISTMAS RETAIL SEASON.... AND IT'S GOING TO TAKE ME **ONE** OF THEM TO STRAIGHTEN ALL THE SHELVES YOU JUST PICKED OVER !!!

OKAY, I'LL BUY THIS, BUT I NEED IT ENGRAVED BY TONIGHT SO I CAN LOOK AT IT FOR TWO DAYS AND DECIDE IF I WANT TO RETURN IT.
GET OUT OF MY STORE!!

SOME OF US WEREN'T MEANT TO SHOP IN FRIENDLY LITTLE BOUTIQUES.
VAL

THIS IS A GREAT GIFT FOR THAT SPECIAL MAN!
THAT? OH, NO. THE DISPLAY IS TOO BIG.
VALENTINES FOR HIM
$49.99
VALENT

THE DISPLAY IS TOO BIG?
TOO BIG. TOO OBVIOUS. HE MIGHT HAVE SEEN IT.
VALENT

I DON'T WANT HIM TO BE ABLE TO TELL WHERE I GOT IT, HOW MUCH I PAID FOR IT, OR THAT ANYONE ELSE HAS EVER THOUGHT OF GIVING IT! IN SHORT, I WANT SOMETHING THAT'S TOTALLY HIDDEN FROM PUBLIC VIEW!!

EXHAUSTED YET UNDAUNTED, THE IN-STORE VALENTINE PROMOTION TEAM MUSTERS ONE FINAL BURST OF CREATIVITY...
VALENTINES

"TO MY ONE TRUE LOVE".... ..YES! WHY NOT?! "TO MY DEAREST DARLING"... YES! "TO MY BELOVED ... MY HEART'S DESIRE"... YES! EMOTIONAL RISK! GO FOR IT! WHY NOT?!
VALENTINES
BE MINE

Sigh...

THE BOTTOM DRAWER OF MY DESK RECEIVES SIX MORE HEARTFELT VALENTINES....
Guisewite

"THE MOST ROMANTIC VALENTINE I'VE EVER RECEIVED IS..."
A SMOKE DETECTOR!
HA, HA! I CAN TOP THAT! A TRAVEL IRON!!

"THE MOST ROMANTIC THING EVER SAID TO ME ON VALENTINE'S DAY IS..."
"REALLY?? IT'S VALENTINE'S DAY??"
"OOPS!" HA, HA! HE JUST SAYS "OOPS!"

SIMON SENT A SINGING CUPID TO MY OFFICE TO INVITE ME TO BE HIS VALENTINE IN A RESTAURANT HE RENTED JUST FOR THE TWO OF US! I THINK HE'S GOING TO PROPOSE!!

NOTHING RUINS A GOOD LAUGH LIKE A LITTLE HAPPINESS.

A DIGITAL MEAT THERMOMETER !!!

SHE WAS EXPECTING AN ENGAGEMENT RING FOR VALENTINE'S DAY, AND HE GAVE HER A DIGITAL MEAT THERMOMETER.
AND I HAD TO ACT HAPPY!

WELL, I AM NOT HAPPY! I WANT MY RING !! I TOLD EVERYONE I WAS GETTING A RING !!

WHAT AM I SUPPOSED TO DO, STRAP A MEAT THER-MOMETER TO MY FINGER ?!
DON'T ASK ME. I SPENT THE MORNING TRY-ING TO MAKE EARRINGS OUT OF MY VALENTINE DUSTBUSTER.

I THOUGHT YOU AND SIMON HAD PICKED OUT A RING TOGETHER, CHARLENE.
I DIDN'T SAY "PICKED OUT." I SAID WE **LOOKED AT** RINGS TOGETHER.

STILL, YOU **LOOKED AT** RINGS TOGETHER.
WELL, NOT "LOOKED AT", EXACTLY. WE **SAW** RINGS TOGETHER.

"SAW"?
OKAY, FINE. WE WERE IN THE CAR, BUT AS WE SPED PAST A JEW-ELERS, HE GLANCED TO THE LEFT AND WE DEFINITELY MIGHT HAVE BOTH SEEN RINGS, WHICH I WAS SURE HE'D GO BACK AND BUY ME ONE OF FOR VALENTINE'S DAY!

DID YOU GIVE ANY OTHER HINTS THAT YOU WERE PLAN-NING TO BECOME ENGAGED TO HIM?
WHAT DO I HAVE TO DO?? WRITE IT OUT IN STONE?!

sniff... it's... it's...
NO, CHARLENE! NOT TODAY! WE DON'T HAVE TIME FOR A LOVE-LIFE CRISIS TODAY!

sniff... it's... sniff...
WE JUST GOT THROUGH CATHY'S CAR CRISIS, MARVIN'S NANNY CRISIS, AND WE'RE RIGHT IN THE MIDDLE OF THE GULF CRISIS...

WE CAN'T HANDLE A LOVE-LIFE CRISIS, TOO! PLEASE!! I'M BEGGING YOU! SUPPRESS IT! HOLD IT BACK! WE HAVE TO GET SOMETHING DONE TODAY..
IT'S OVER WITH SIMON!!!

OUR OFFICE: UNITED IN ALL CAUSES EXCEPT THOSE THAT INVOLVE DOING ANY WORK.

WHAT HAPPENED, CHARLENE?
I DON'T KNOW. SIMON JUST STARTED GETTING WEIRD. THEN I STARTED GETTING WEIRD.

THEN HE GOT EVEN WEIRDER. THEN I GOT EVEN WEIRDER.

THEN HE GOT EVEN WEIRDER THAN THAT! THEN I GOT EVEN WEIRDER THAN HE GOT! THEN HE GOT EVEN WEIRDER THAN I GOT! THEN I GOT WEIRDER... THEN... THEN...

...ALL THAT'S LEFT OF US AS A COUPLE IS OUR COMPETITIVE SPIRIT.

SIMON'S GOING TO PACK UP MY STUFF AND BRING IT OVER, CATHY.
GOOD. IT WILL MAKE HIM FEEL TERRIBLE.
CHARLENE

IMAGINE HIM GATHERING UP YOUR SILKY BATHROBE...
I DIDN'T LEAVE A ROBE.
YOUR FAVORITE COLOGNE...
NO COLOGNE.
LACY LINGERIE...
SWEATPANTS, RICE CAKES AND "FEMALE SUPPLIES."

I DIDN'T LEAVE ANY GOOD STUFF! **HIS LAST IMAGE OF ME IS GOING TO BE A BAG OF ICKY STUFF!!!**

...WHAT'S ALL THAT, CATHY?
NOTHING, IRVING. REALLY... AHEM... ..DON'T GET UP...

WHY DON'T YOU AND SIMON GO BACK TO THE THERAPIST, CHARLENE ?
I'M TOO OLD TO KEEP RE-HASHING A RELATIONSHIP THAT DOESN'T WORK, CATHY.

FOR ONCE IN MY LIFE, I AM GOING TO BE TOTALLY REALIS-TIC ABOUT MY WANTS AND NEEDS AND FIND A MAN WHO IS APPROPRIATE TO MY LIFE-STYLE FROM DAY ONE !!
WANTS
NEEDS

ARTHUR KENT, WAR CORRESPONDENT.

"DO HIS ENDEARING LITTLE HABITS NOW NAUSEATE YOU?"

YES!

I HAVE FLUNKED MY RELATIONSHIP, BUT I FINALLY PASSED A QUIZ.

GREAT RELATIONSHIPS TAKE TIME, CHARLENE! LOOK AT IRVING AND ME!
WHERE? I DON'T SEE IRVING.

YOU KNOW WHAT I MEAN. LOOK AT US AS A COUPLE!
WHAT COUPLE? HE'S AT HIS HOUSE. YOU'RE HERE.

WHERE'S THE COUPLE?? IF YOU WANT TO BE MY ROLE MODEL AS A COUPLE, SHOW ME TWO PEOPLE IN THE ROOM AT THE SAME TIME!!

I HAVE A PHOTO OF HIM IN THE DRAWER. CLOSE ENOUGH.
AH. NOW THERE'S SOMETHING TO SHOOT FOR.

MORE CONTAGIOUS THAN THE COMMON COLD...MORE DEBILITATING THAN THE FLU... ...BARRELING UN-CHECKED THROUGH THE OFFICES OF CORPORATE AMERICA....

WELL, IT ISN'T **PERFECT** WITH JOE, CHARLENE. SOMETIMES I FEEL A LITTLE JEALOUS...
JEALOUSY ISN'T ENOUGH TO RUIN A RELATIONSHIP, MARGO.
COFFEE ROOM

SOMETIMES I FEEL PRETTY INSECURE...
INSECURITY ISN'T ENOUGH TO RUIN A RELATIONSHIP.

SOMETIMES I FEEL TAKEN FOR GRANTED, BUT WHEN YOU PUT THEM ALL TOGETHER, I GUESS I...WELL...I...I....

I FEEL STUPID!
BINGO! BREAK UP!
BRING IN THE TISSUES. THE GODDESS OF DOOM JUST TRASHED ANOTHER ONE.

WE'RE HAPPY, AREN'T WE, IRVING?
OF COURSE WE'RE HAPPY, CATHY.

THERE'S THIS BREAK-UP VIRUS GOING AROUND THE OFFICE, AND I JUST NEED TO MAKE SURE WE'RE REALLY HAPPY.
WE'RE REALLY HAPPY.

ARE WE REALLY **REALLY** HAPPY, OR ARE YOU JUST PRETENDING YOU'RE HAPPY BECAUSE I SEEM SO HAPPY AND YOU DON'T WANT TO TELL ME YOU'RE NOT HAPPY?

...**AACK!!** PARANOIA!! THE FIRST SYMPTOM!
WHY DID YOU ASK? AREN'T YOU REALLY HAPPY?

I BROUGHT HOME FOUR REPORTS TO WRITE. DIDN'T TOUCH THEM.

I BROUGHT HOME THREE POUNDS OF READING MATERIAL. DIDN'T GLANCE AT IT.

I BROUGHT HOME ONE TEENSY QUESTION ABOUT MY RELATIONSHIP. IT FILLED UP MY WHOLE HOUSE, CONTAMINATED EVERY SPECK OF AIR, PLASTERED ITSELF ALL OVER EVERY SURFACE AND MUTILATED MY EVENING.

IF ONLY BRAINS COULD BE STUFFED INTO BRIEFCASES SO WE'D NEVER BE TEMPTED TO LOOK AT THEM...

IRVING CALLED ME OVEREMOTIONAL.

HE SAID I WAS AN IRRATIONAL, HYSTERICAL, HORMONE-CRAZED LOONIE, AND THEN HE STOMPED OUT THE DOOR!!

THEY ALWAYS LEAVE JUST WHEN THEY REALLY GET TO KNOW YOU.

HI, SWEETIE. IT'S MOM. HOW WAS YOUR WEEK?
FINE.
diet

UH, OH. WHEN YOU SAY IT WAS FINE, IT MEANS YOU'RE NOT TALKING, SO I HAVE TO ASSUME IT WAS TERRIBLE.

I ONLY KNOW YOUR WEEK WAS OKAY IF YOU SAY IT WAS AW-FUL, BECAUSE THEN I KNOW YOU'VE COPED WITH IT, GOT-TEN OVER IT, AND AREN'T TRYING TO KEEP ANYTHING FROM YOUR MOTHER.
OKAY! MY WEEK WAS AW-FUL, MOM!

OH, POOR BABY! I'LL BE RIGHT OVER!!

I CAN'T LIVE WITH-OUT SIMON!! I CAN'T LIVE WITH-OUT SIMON!!
THAT DOES IT, CHAR-LENE.

JUST PICK UP THE PHONE, MAKE THE CALL, AND GET IT OVER WITH!

I SIGNED UP FOR VIDEO DATING!! I SIGNED UP FOR VIDEO DATING!!

ONLY TIME CAN HEAL A BROKEN HEART, BUT HUMILIATION CAN TAKE YOUR MIND OFF IT FOR A WHILE.

WHY DON'T YOU LET ME FIX YOU UP, CHARLENE?
BECAUSE I'LL JUST GET MY HOPES UP, MEET HIM AND BE REVOLTED.

ONLY VIDEO DATING GIVES ME THE CHANCE TO REJECT A MAN STRICTLY BECAUSE OF HOW HE LOOKS WITHOUT HAVING TO SPEND ONE SECOND PRETENDING I'M NOT THAT TACKY!

BUT CHARLENE, ANY **MAN** WHO'S SIGNED UP FOR VIDEO DATING IS TACKY ENOUGH TO REJECT **YOU** ON LOOKS, TOO!

I KNOW. AT LEAST WE'LL GO INTO IT KNOWING WE HAVE ONE THING IN COMMON.

PLEASE, CATHY... I'M TOO NERVOUS TO GO INTO THE VIDEO-DATING PLACE ALL BY MYSELF.
FORGET IT, CHARLENE. I AM NOT GOING TO HELP YOU MAKE A FOOL OF YOURSELF!
VIDEO MATE
VIDEO MATE

THIS IS THE WORST IDEA YOU EVER HAD! I WANT NO PART OF IT! I DO NOT SUPPORT IT! I DO NOT ENDORSE IT!!
VIDEO MATE

I RESENT YOU FOR EVEN MAKING ME BE ON THIS SIDEWALK, BREATHING THE SAME AIR THE BUILDING IS IN!!!

IF WE DON'T HAVE SOMEONE TO LEAN ON, WE AT LEAST NEED SOMEONE TO DRAG...

THE BEAUTY OF VIDEO DATING IS THAT YOU CAN PRESELECT A MATE WHO YOU KNOW SHARES YOUR HOBBIES AND INTERESTS.
VIDEO♥MATE
SIGN UP!

WE HAVE THE SPORTY TYPE...
THE ARTY TYPE...
THE BRAINY TYPE...
THE CUDDLY TYPE...
JUST TELL US WHAT YOU WANT!
SPORTY
ARTY

I WANT TO GET BACK AT THE MAN WHO RUINED MY LIFE!!!

AH! OUR BIGGEST CATEGORY! THE REVENGE-Y TYPE!
REVENGE-Y

FEEL FREE TO STOP IN THE LADIES ROOM WHILE WE SET UP TO MAKE YOUR VIDEO-TAPE, CHARLENE.
NO, THANKS. THIS IS HOW I AM! TAKE IT OR LEAVE IT!
VIDEO ♡ MATE

...WELL, MAYBE JUST A DAB OF LIPSTICK. BUT THAT'S IT. NO CAMOUFLAGE! NO HOCUS-POCUS!
DIES

...OKAY, MAYBE JUST A TEENSY BIT OF CONCEALER... MAYBE JUST A TOUCH OF BLUSH...A LITTLE EYELINER....

...AND GEL! I NEED GEL!! BRING ME GEL AND A STYLING WAND!!
JUST POINT THE CAMERA AT THE DOOR. IT'S ALL ANY MAN WILL EVER SEE OF HER ANYWAY.
LADIES

JUST RELAX AND TALK ABOUT WHAT YOU'RE LOOKING FOR IN A RELA-TIONSHIP.
I DON'T WANT TO SOUND TOO AVAILABLE.
VIDEO MATE

THIS IS A VIDEO DATING SER-VICE, CHARLENE. YOU'RE **SUP**-POSED TO SOUND AVAILABLE.

HI! MY NAME IS CHARLENE. YOU CAN'T HAVE ME! DON'T EVEN TRY! I'M ALREADY IN-VOLVED! OFF THE MARKET! **LEAVE ME ALONE!!!**
VIDEO MATE

CUT!
SORRY. FORCE OF HABIT.
THE CAMERA-MAN WANTS YOUR PHONE NUMBER.
VIDEO MATE

SHE WATCHES...
THIS IS CHARLENE! TAKE 87!
HI! I'M HEE HEE HEE HEE...
VIDEO MATE "Charlene"
VIDEO MATE

SHE REELS...
HEE HEE HOO HA HEE HA
OH, FOR CRYING OUT LOUD, CHARLENE! WE'VE BEEN HERE FOR THREE HOURS!
VIDEO MATE

...AND IN THE FINAL CLASSIC TANGLE OF HORROR AND SELF-CONFIDENCE, SHE REALIZES SHE'S NOT ONLY WATCHING THE MOST IDIOTIC THING SHE'S EVER SEEN...

...BUT THAT SHE'D BE BETTER AT IT.
...MOVE OVER.
HI! I'M CATHY!
Guisewite

BRAVO, CATHY! YOU'RE A PERFECT VIDEO DATE!
ME?? OH, NO! I WAS JUST SHOWING CHARLENE HOW IT'S DONE SO WE COULD GET OUT OF HERE!
VIDEO MATE

YOU WERE SO WITTY! YOU WERE SO CHARMING!
FORGET IT!
VIDEO♥MATE
CATHY

VIDEO DATING IS NOT ONLY THE MOST REPULSIVE ACT OF DESPERATION I'VE EVER HEARD OF, BUT VIOLATES EVERY VALUE I HOLD DEAR!!

YOU LOOK SKINNY ON CAMERA, CATHY.
UH-OH.
ARTY LIGHTING CASTS ANOTHER SHADOW ON THE MORAL HIGH GROUND...

I CAN'T SIGN UP FOR VIDEO DATING! I HAVE A BOYFRIEND!!
I LOOKED STUNNING ON CAMERA...

I CAN'T SIGN UP FOR VIDEO DATING! I DON'T BELIEVE IN IT!!
MEN WILL LUST AFTER ME...

CONTRACT

ONCE AGAIN, THE EGO SHOWS UP JUST LONG ENOUGH TO CONVINCE ME TO TOTALLY HUMILIATE MYSELF....
VIDEO
MATE
CONTRACT

I KNOW, I KNOW...THE "OVERLY-PICKY-BIOLOGICAL-CLOCKERS" NEVER WANT TO DATE CLICHÉS.

VIDEO♥MATE

YOU'RE NOT LOOKING AT ANY OF THE MEN I PICKED OUT FOR YOU.
IT JUST SEEMS SO PERSONAL. WOULDN'T THEY BE EMBARRASSED TO KNOW I WAS WATCHING THEIR TAPES?

CATHY, ALL THOSE MEN SIGNED UP HOPING THEY'D MEET A WOMAN AS SENSITIVE AND CARING AS YOU...HERE. I'LL CLOSE THE DOOR SO YOU CAN GIVE THEM THE PRIVACY AND RESPECT YOU TREASURE SO HIGHLY.

VIDEO♥MATE
VIEWING ROOM

...AND I LOVE A TIDY SOCK DRAWER...
COME IN HERE, CHARLENE! GET A LOAD OF THIS ONE!!

CHARLENE FORCED ME TO GO TO THE VIDEO-DATING PLACE WITH HER, AND SOMEHOW I WOUND UP HAVING A TAPE MADE OF **MYSELF**, ELECTRA!
diet

OF COURSE, I DIDN'T MAKE THE TAPE ON **PURPOSE**... I WAS JUST SHOWING HER HOW TO DO IT, AND THEY ACCIDENTALLY MADE ONE OF ME!

IT'S NOTHING I WOULD EVER REALLY **DO**... OKAY, I **DID** IT... BUT JUST BY ACCIDENT, SO EVEN THOUGH I WENT AHEAD AND SIGNED UP, IT ISN'T AS THOUGH I'M **REALLY**...HA...HA...

WE KNOW WE'RE IN TROUBLE WHEN IT DOESN'T EVEN SOUND GOOD BEING EXPLAINED TO A DOG.
diet
GUISEWITE

THINGS TO NEVER TRY EXPLAINING TO A MAN:

1. WHY SOCIAL EVENTS HAVE TO BE CANCELED FOR SIX WEEKS IF YOUR BANGS GET CUT 1/8 INCH TOO SHORT.

2. THE EFFECT THAT ONE FLUORESCENT LIGHT IN A DRESSING ROOM CAN HAVE ON ALL FUTURE PHYSICAL ACTIVITY WITH HIM.

3. THE DIFFERENCE BETWEEN THE NINE SHADES OF TAUPE EYESHADOW IN YOUR BATHROOM.

4. THE DIFFERENCE BETWEEN THE 16 PAIRS OF BLACK SHOES IN YOUR CLOSET.

5. THE DIFFERENCE BETWEEN TAKING 25 BITES OF HIS PIE VS. ORDERING ONE OF YOUR OWN.

6. ANY IDEA EVER SUGGESTED BY A SINGLE GIRLFRIEND.

I TOLD IRVING I SIGNED UP FOR VIDEO DATING AND NOW HE ISN'T SPEAKING TO ME, CHAR-LENE. I HOPE YOU'RE HAPPY.
RECEPTIONIS

I AM! I TOLD SIMON I SIGNED UP FOR VIDEO DATING AND HE BEGGED ME TO COME BACK TO HIM, SO I CAN-CELED MY MEMBERSHIP!!

YOU CANCELED?? YOU DRAGGED ME INTO THIS, DESTROYED MY RELATIONSHIP, AND NOW YOU'RE LEAVING ME ALL ALONE?!!
OH, YOU WON'T BE ALONE, CATHY.

VIDEO-MATE ALREADY CALLED AND HAS FOUR LIVE ONES WHO ARE PANTING TO MEET YOU!
RECEPTIONIST

HI. I'M ROD. I'VE GOT THE PORSCHE WITH A PHONE, THE PAD WITH A VIEW... NOW ALL I NEED IS A CLASSY LADY LIKE YOU!
AACK!

HI. I'M CARL. I'M INTO FEELINGS. YOUR FEELINGS. MY FEELINGS. OUR FEELINGS. YOUR FEELINGS ABOUT OUR FEELINGS. MY FEELINGS ABOUT...
AACK!!

HI. I'M BERNIE.
AAACK!!
BAM BAM

HI. I'M CATHY. I WANT MY MONEY BACK.
VIDEO♥MAT

THESE WERE NOT THE MEN I PICKED! WHERE ARE THE MEN I PICKED??
NONE OF THE MEN YOU PICKED PICKED YOU.
VIDEO♥MATE

THE MEN I PICKED CAME IN, LOOKED AT MY TAPE AND DIDN'T PICK ME??

THE SAME MEN WHO WERE "SEARCHING FOR A WOMAN OF DEPTH AND SENSITIVITY" REJECTED ME ON THE BASIS OF A THREE-MINUTE VIDEOTAPE??

YOU DIDN'T EVEN LOOK AT THIS ONE, CATHY.
I DON'T LIKE THE WAY HIS NAME IS TYPED ON THE BOX.
VIDEO♥MATE
Guisewite

HI, SWEETIE. HOW'S IT GOING?
JUST GREAT, MOTHER.

IN THE LAST WEEK, I HAVE SUBJECTED MYSELF TO THE LOWEST FORM OF DEGRADATION...

I HAVE PUT MY EGO ON THE LINE AND HAD IT SQUASHED... ...I HAVE WADDED UP WHAT WAS LEFT OF MY SELF-ESTEEM AND FLUNG IT RIGHT DOWN THE SEWER!

SHE'S DATING AGAIN!!
Guisewite

I'LL JUST CALL IRVING AND SAY IT WAS ALL SO SILLY...
((POOF POOF))
((PRIMP PRIMP))

JUST A SILLY LITTLE MISUNDERSTANDING...WE'LL LAUGH... WE'LL TALK...WE'LL BE CLOSER THAN EVER...
((VACUUM VACUUM))

HI. THIS IS IRVING. PLEASE LEAVE A MESSAGE AT THE BEEP...

OLDER, WISER...BUT STILL DOING MAKEOVERS FOR AN ANSWERING MACHINE....
Guisewite

MR. PINKLEY, YOU'VE HAD A PACKAGE AT THE FRONT DESK FOR TWO HOURS! PLEASE COME TO THE FRONT DESK!!

BRIAN, THIS IS YOUR FIFTH PAGE! PICK UP YOUR MESSAGES AT THE FRONT DESK!!!

CATHY, YOU HAVE A CALL FROM A VIDEO DATE AT THE FRONT DESK.

THE URBAN VULTURES: OBLIVIOUS TO ALL EXCEPT THE SCENT OF FRESH POPCORN OR DECAYING DIGNITY.

IS IT WORSE TO MEET HIM IN A RESTAURANT AND HAVE A ROOMFUL OF TOTAL STRANGERS STARING AT US DURING OUR "GETTING TO KNOW YOU" MEAL...

OR IS IT WORSE TO MEET HIM IN THE PRIVACY OF MY HOME AND HAVE A POTENTIAL PSYCHO-PATH KNOW WHERE I LIVE ?

EMBARRASSMENT OR DEATH. ALWAYS A TOUGH CALL, CATHY.

EVEN WHEN I KNOW WHO I'M GOING TO BE WITH, THERE'S NO DECENT WAY TO MEET A MAN!!!

I ACCEPTED A DATE WITH A MAN I KNOW NOTHING ABOUT EX-CEPT WHAT I SAW ON HIS THREE-MINUTE "VIDEO-MATE" TAPE, MOTHER.
HAVE A NICE TIME, DEAR.

"HAVE A NICE TIME"?? THAT'S IT?
CATHY, YOUR FATHER AND I SUPPORT YOU IN THIS JUST AS WE SUPPORT YOU IN ALL THINGS.

NO MATTER WHAT YOU DO OR WHERE YOU GO, WE ARE ALWAYS HERE FOR YOU!

...QUIETLY RIPPING OUR HAIR OUT.

WHEW, BOY! I HATE FIRST DATES!
I HATE PEOPLE WHO SAY THEY HATE FIRST DATES ON THE FIRST DATE.

I HATE THE AWKWARDNESS... HATE THE FORMALITY...
I HATE HAVING THE SAME STUPID CONVERSATION.

I HATE THAT WHOLE "TRYING-TO-GUESS-IF-IT'S-GOING-ANYWHERE" THING.
I HATE THIS RESTAURANT. I HATE HIM. I HATE MYSELF.

BRING THE MENUS! LET'S GET THIS OVER WITH!!
I HATE FIRST DATES...

HOWARD! WHAT A COINCIDENCE!
...A SPY?? YOU HAD A FRIEND COME SPY ON ME??

...WELL, I JUST...
WHAT IS THIS, JUNIOR HIGH?? WHAT AM I, A SIDE SHOW??!

I'M SORRY, I JUST...
FORGET IT! IF I'M GOING TO BE SPIED UPON, AT LEAST GIVE ME A MOMENT TO POWDER MY NOSE!!
LADIES

HE COULD BE CUTE WITH DIF-FERENT HAIR.
TOTAL GEEK.
I'LL TAKE HIM!
YOU COULD DO WORSE, DEAR.
EXIT

I GUESS YOU DIDN'T HAVE A VERY GOOD TIME WITH ME, CATHY.
OH, NO. DON'T START WORKING ON MY EMOTIONS.
VALET PARKING
WAIT HERE

I KNOW I WAS SILLY TO THINK A WOMAN AS PRETTY AS YOU COULD LIKE SOMEONE LIKE ME.
DON'T DO THIS TO ME. DON'T SAY IT! DON'T SAY IT! DON'T...

I EVEN BOUGHT A BRAND-NEW SUIT TO IMPRESS YOU.
AAUGH !! OKAY! LET'S HAVE DINNER AGAIN NEXT WEEK!!

REALLY??
IF MEN DON'T HAVE A COSMOPOLITAN MAGAZINE, WHERE DO THEY LEARN HOW TO DO THIS TO US???
ALET
KING
WAIT
HERE

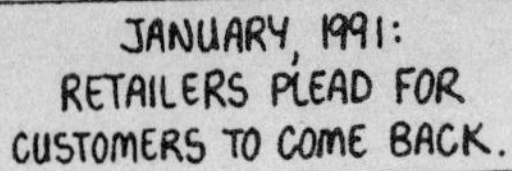
JANUARY, 1991:
RETAILERS PLEAD FOR CUSTOMERS TO COME BACK.

COME BACK!
SALE
SALE

FEBRUARY, 1991:
RETAILERS PRAY FOR CUSTOMERS TO COME BACK.
PLEASE COME BACK!
BIG SALE
BIG SALE

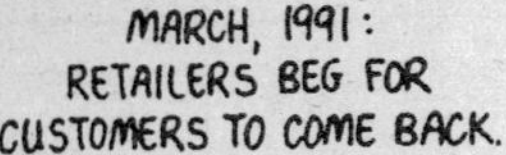
MARCH, 1991:
RETAILERS BEG FOR CUSTOMERS TO COME BACK.

PLEASE, PRETTY PLEASE, COME BACK!
HUGE SALE
HUGE SALE

APRIL, 1991:
CUSTOMERS COME BACK.
I MIGHT GET THIS IF YOU SPECIAL ORDER IT IN BLUE AND ALTER IT FOR ME FOR FREE BEFORE I REALLY DECIDE.
GO AWAY.

THIS SPRING, NOTHING SAYS SO MUCH ABOUT A WOMAN AS A DRESS!
I LOVE DRESSES!

FOR WOMEN WITH BIG BUSTS AND NO REARS, THE CLASSIC SHEATH DRESS...FOR WOMEN WITH BIG REARS AND NO BUSTS, THE TRAPEZE DRESS!
DRESSE

BOTH IN WILD, EYE-POPPING NEON COLORS, SO PEOPLE WILL KNOW YOUR EXACT FIGURE TYPE FROM UP TO A HALF-MILE AWAY!
WHERE ARE YOUR PANTS?

DID YOU WANT THE "PERFECT THIGH" SPANDEX LEGGINGS... OR THE "I-SPENT-MY-HEALTH-CLUB-MONEY-ON-CHEESECAKE" BAGGY TROUSERS?
Guisewite

OF COURSE THAT LOOKS DRAB. YOU NEED ACCESSORIES!

THE PSEUDO-SILVER CUFFS...
THE CHUNKY ERSATZ PEARLS...
THE SIMULATED ETHNIC BEADS...
THE ARTIFICIAL GOLD CHAINS...
THE MOCK-JEWEL EARRINGS...

PUT IT ALL TOGETHER AND SEE WHAT YOU HAVE ??!

THE FAUX-WOMAN.
WITH, I MIGHT ADD, THE BOGUS CREDIT LINE.
NEXT!

THE WOMEN OF THIS COUNTRY REJECTED THE MINI-SKIRT FOR THE LAST THREE YEARS. CAN'T YOU TAKE A HINT ??
YES! TA, DA! WE MADE THEM EVEN SHORTER!
MINI

EVERY TIME YOU DON'T BUY THE MINIS, WE TAKE THEM TO OUR BACK ROOM AND CHOP ANOTHER THREE INCHES OFF THE HEM!

IGNORE THE MINIS FOR ONE MORE SEASON, AND THERE WILL ONLY BE TWO INCHES OF FABRIC LEFT, WHICH WE'LL TRIM WITH ELASTIC AND STITCH UP INTO THE SWIMWEAR LINE OF YOUR NIGHTMARES!!

WE'RE BUYING MINI-SKIRTS, CHARLENE.
THE CONCEPT OF "INVESTMENT SHOPPING" IS FINALLY CATCHING ON.

I COULD WEAR THIS, BUT I'D HAVE TO IRON THE BLOUSE THAT GOES WITH IT...

I AM NOT IRONING A BLOUSE TODAY! I DON'T HAVE TIME TO IRON A BLOUSE TODAY!!

I DON'T CARE IF I HAVE TO TRY ON EVERY STUPID THING IN THIS CLOSET! I AM NOT GOING TO WASTE FIVE MIN-UTES OF MY VALUABLE TIME IRONING A BLOUSE!!!

CATHY'S RUNNING A FEW HOURS LATE, MR. PINKLEY... SHE'S SPENDING THE MORNING NOT IRONING ANYTHING.
RECEPTIONIST

"SIXTIES DRESSING WITH A NEW TWIST." WHAT'S THE NEW TWIST?
THE NEW TWIST IS THAT A "FLOWER-POWER" TUNIC NOW COSTS $300!
SIXTIES DRESSING WITH A NEW TWIST

THE VERY STYLES THAT DEFINED A WHOLE DECADE OF REBELLION AGAINST CAPITALISM ARE NOW BEING CHARGED ON EX-HIPPIES' PLATINUM AMERICAN EXPRESS CARDS FOR $300 A POP!
SIXTIES DRESSING WITH A NEW TWIST

AMERICA IS ALIVE AND WELL! LONG LIVE AMERICA!!

LET'S GO LOOK AT SHOES.
CHECK OUT THE $400 SATIN PEACE SYMBOL WEDGIES! THEY'RE PERFECT WITH OUR $275 SHREDDED DENIMS!!
SIXTIES DRESSING WITH A NEW TWIST

JANUARY, 1990: $425 THROWN AWAY ON WORKOUT EQUIPMENT I DIDN'T USE...
MARCH, 1990: $250 THROWN AWAY ON SHOES I DIDN'T NEED...
TAX STUFF

MAY, 1990: $68 THROWN AWAY ON PLANTS I MURDERED...
JULY, 1990: $133 THROWN AWAY ON SELF-IMPROVEMENT BOOKS I DIDN'T READ...
TAX STUFF

SEPTEMBER, 1990: $85 THROWN AWAY ON A HAIRDO I HATED...
NOVEMBER, 1990: $100 THROWN AWAY ON FOOD I THREW AWAY...
TAX STUFF

A DECADE OF FINANCIAL INDEPENDENCE, AND THE ONLY CONCEPT I'VE TRULY MASTERED IS THAT OF "DISPOSABLE INCOME."

I THOUGHT MY FINANCIAL DISASTER OF LAST YEAR WAS SOCIETY'S FAULT...

I THOUGHT IT WAS THE PRESIDENT'S FAULT...MY MOTHER'S FAULT...MY BOYFRIEND'S FAULT... ...MY BOSS'S FAULT....

...BUT NOW--IN THE QUIET, DARK AND LONELY STILL OF THE NIGHT--I HAVE TO FACE WHAT I SHOULD HAVE SEEN ALL ALONG...
TAX WORKBOOK

IT'S MY ACCOUNTANT'S FAULT !!!
...HUH?
BOLT THE DOORS, DEAR. ANOTHER CLIENT JUST OPENED HER WORKBOOK...

TO LOOK "OFFICE ACCEPTABLE", A MAN NEEDS A $200 SUIT, $60 SHOES, A $30 SHIRT, $5 OF UNDERWEAR AND A $10 HAIRCUT.
MEN
ACCOUNTANT

TO LOOK "OFFICE ACCEPTABLE," A WOMAN NEEDS A $200 SUIT, $80 SHOES, A $90 BLOUSE, $35 OF LINGERIE, A $45 HAIRCUT, $5 PANTYHOSE, $46 OF MAKEUP, A $10 MANICURE, $200 OF JEWELRY, AND A $30 PURSE CONTAINING $9 OF EMERGENCY SUPPLIES TO MAINTAIN HER "PROFESSIONAL LOOK" THROUGHOUT THE DAY.
WOMEN

THUS, ON BEHALF OF ALL WOMEN, I DEMAND A YEAR-END REFUND FOR EACH OF US, PLUS $10 PER HOUR FOR ALL THE EXTRA SHOPPING TIME REQUIRED!

IT ALL EVENS OUT WITH THE EXTRA ASPIRIN MEN HAVE TO BUY.
MEDICINE IS A DIFFERENT CATEGORY. SHALL I BEGIN WITH OUR THERAPY BILLS?...
MEDICIN
MEN
WOMEN
ACCOUNTANT

I'M DEDUCTING ALL MY SUITS AS A BUSINESS EXPENSE.
SUITS AREN'T DEDUCTIBLE. YOU CAN WEAR THEM FOR PLEASURE.
ACCOUNTANT

TO WEAR A SUIT FOR "PLEASURE," A WOMAN HAS TO BUY A LACY CAMISOLE, DRESSY PUMPS, EVENING BAG, CHUNKY JEWELRY AND COORDINATING PANTYHOSE!

IF WE'RE GOING TO SPEND $500, IT'S NOT GOING TO BE TO ACCESSORIZE THE SUITS WE'VE WORN UNTIL 9:00 EVERY NIGHT WORKING LATE AT THE STUPID OFFICE!!
YOU'VE WORN YOUR SUITS UNTIL 9:00 AT THE OFFICE?

VOILÀ! EVENING WEAR! NOT DEDUCTIBLE.
ACCOUNTANT

"WHITE LEGGINGS." NOT DEDUCTIBLE.
THE LEGGINGS WERE A FASHION BLUNDER. THEY WERE NEVER WORN.
TAX WORKSHEET
ACCOUNTANT

BY ALLOWING MYSELF TO BE TALKED INTO THOSE LEGGINGS, I WAS FORCED TO FACE EVERY INSECURITY AND RECHANNEL THE ANGST INTO A MORE FORCEFUL AND CONFIDENT PERSONA!
TAX WORKSHEET

THE PERSONA ALLOWS ME TO BE BETTER AT MY JOB... WHICH ALLOWS ME TO POUR MORE BACK INTO THE ECONOMY... WHICH SECURES COUNTLESS JOBS AND KEEPS WHO KNOWS HOW MANY PEOPLE'S LITTLE CHILDREN HAPPY AND WELL FED!!

"PURPLE LINGERIE." NOT DEDUCTIBLE.
THE LINGERIE INCIDENT CARRIED FOUR SEPARATE DOUGHNUT CHAINS THROUGH THE ECONOMIC SLUMP OF 1990.
TAX WORKSHEET

MONEY MAGAZINE HAD 49 DIFFERENT TAX PREPARERS DO THE SAME TAX RETURN AND THEY GOT 49 DIFFERENT ANSWERS... ...RANGING FROM A TAX DUE OF $6807 TO $73,247 !!
Money
ACCOUNTANT

HOW DO I KNOW YOU'RE NOT ALL JUST GUESSING?? HOW DO I KNOW SOMEONE ELSE WOULDN'T HAVE GUESSED LOWER??
ACCOUNTA

PLEASE...GIVE ME A SHRED OF REASSURANCE... TELL ME SOMETHING TO MAKE ME FEEL BETTER!
IF YOU POP YOUR RETURN IN THE MAIL RIGHT NOW, YOU WON'T HAVE TO THINK ABOUT IT FOR A YEAR.

AH.
OH, HOW THE WORLD LOVES AN HONEST ACCOUNTANT....
ACCOUNTANT

MY TAXES WIPED ME OUT! WHAT AM I GOING TO DO??
ACCEPT THE FACT THAT YOU'RE WAL-LOWING IN THE WASTELAND OF YOUR OWN MAKING AND MOVE ON, MR. PINKLEY!

HUH?
TODAY IS A NEW DAY! EVERY MOMENT YOU DON'T BLOW IT AS BADLY AS YOU BLEW IT BE-FORE IS A VICTORY!

IF YOU'VE EVEN MADE IT TO 9:00 THIS MORNING WITHOUT ANY OF YOUR USUAL BLUNDERS, YOU'VE SCORED A RICH, PER-SONAL TRIUMPH! A BUILDING BLOCK TOWARD THE NEW YOU!

...UH, THANKS, CATHY...
IF 15 YEARS OF DIETING HAVE TAUGHT ME ANY-THING, IT'S HOW TO START OVER.

WHO WILL STAY LATE TO FINISH THIS?

I HAVE TO PICK UP JOSH AT PRE-SCHOOL.
I HAVE TO TAKE JENNY TO BALLET.
I HAVE TO CARPOOL JAKE'S LITTLE LEAGUE.
I HAVE TO MAKE DINNER FOR JULIE.

I HAVE TO MEET SOMEONE, FALL IN LOVE, GET MARRIED, SET UP HOUSE, GET PREGNANT AND GIVE BIRTH!!!

HAVE IT ON MY DESK BY MORNING, CATHY.
IF PARENTS CAN LEAVE AT 5:00, SINGLE PEOPLE SHOULD GET TO GO HOME AT NOON.

HELLO, WOMEN'S DEPARTMENT? AHEM...IS MABEL WORKING TODAY?
YES. MAY I SAY WHO'S....

SLAM!
UNBELIEVABLE! I'VE BEEN TRYING TO SNEAK BACK TO RETURN THIS WITH-OUT HAVING TO FACE MY SALES-CLERK AND EVERY TIME I CALL, SHE'S THERE!!
Mall

SUNDAY AFTERNOON...WEDNES-DAY NIGHT...SATURDAY MORN-ING...SHE'S HOLDING A 24-HOUR VIGIL!! SHE'S WAITING FOR ME LIKE A VULTURE!!

MORE OVERTIME THIS WEEK, MABEL?
I ALWAYS LIKE TO BE HERE FOR MY SPECIAL CUSTOMERS.
WOMEN'S

TEN-CAR LINE AT THE "FAST-FOOD" DRIVE-THROUGH...

SIX-CAR LINE FOR THE CARRY-OUT CHINESE FOOD PARKING LOT, AND A 15-PERSON LINE INSIDE...
MENU →

TWELVE-PERSON LINE AT THE EXPRESS CHECK-OUT TO BUY ONE BARBECUED DELI CHICKEN...
EXPRESS
CHIPS

WHATEVER HAPPENED TO THE GOOD OLD DAYS WHEN IT TOOK LESS TIME TO BUY A MEAL THAN TO COOK ONE?
To Go

CHARLENE, WHAT DO YOU MEAN, DUMPING THIS ON MY DESK??
I DUMPED IT ON YOUR DESK BECAUSE GRANT DUMPED IT ON MY DESK.
RECEPTIONIST

GRANT!
I DUMPED IT ON CHARLENE'S DESK BECAUSE MARGO DUMPED IT ON MY DESK.
RECEPTIONIST

MARGO! THIS IMBE-CILIC LITTLE GAME IS GOING TO STOP RIGHT NOW!! WHERE IS MARGO?!
MARGO ISN'T IN TODAY.
RECEPTIONIST

MARGO

I CALLED IRVING 4.6 MORE TIMES THAN HE CALLED ME LAST MONTH. FOR EACH TIME I GOT HIS VOICE-MAIL, I GET TWO EXTRA POINTS. FOR EACH EMOTIONALLY RISKY EVENING CALL, EIGHT EXTRA POINTS.

MEANWHILE, I STAGED SEVEN "RELATIONSHIP EPISODES," WHICH WERE THREE TIMES WORSE THAN THE TWO HE STAGED... WHICH WOULD MAKE US EVEN EXCEPT THE LAST ONE WAS AT HIS HOUSE, GIVING ME NINE BONUS POINTS FOR DRIVING OVER!

THEREFORE, I WIN! IT IS **HIS** TURN TO CALL!!
CATHY, **HE** ISN'T GOING TO KNOW THAT.

IGNORANCE OF THE RULES! TWO DEMERITS! THE NEXT FIVE CALLS ARE HIS!!

MR. PINKLEY! THE FLOWERS YOU SENT ME FOR SECRE-TARIES WEEK ARE GORGEOUS!
THE WHAT? ...AHEM... I WHAT??

LOOK AT THIS ARRANGEMENT! IT MUST HAVE COST A FORTUNE!
...WELL... AHEM.... NOTHING'S TOO GOOD FOR MY SECRETARY.

...AND THE LITTLE CARD YOU ENCLOSED PROMISING ME STOCK OPTIONS AND A BRAND-NEW, BRIGHT-RED MIATA WAS SUCH A SWEET TOUCH!
THUNK!

WHAT DO YOU BET HE'LL RE-MEMBER TO SEND THEM HIMSELF NEXT YEAR?
WILL I GET A FREE PARKING SPOT WITH THIS?

SECRETARIES WORK LIKE MANI-ACS FOR DEADLINES WE CAN'T CHANGE... POLICIES WE CAN'T ALTER...CO-WORKERS WE CAN'T CHOOSE... CLIENTS WE CAN'T YELL AT AND MEETINGS WE CAN'T GO TO!
Secretaries Week

IN SHORT, WE HAVE ALL THE PRESSURES OF BUSINESS WITH NONE OF THE POWER, MAKING OURS THE HIGHEST-STRESS JOB IN THE OFFICE!

OH YEAH?? TRY **MY** JOB!!
Secretaries Week

...AND THE FINAL TORTURE, A DOOR WE CAN'T CLOSE.
Secretaries Week

IT'S SECRETARIES DAY, CHARLENE, AND I JUST WANT TO SAY I KNOW HOW DEMANDING I AM.
HAPPY SECRETARIES DAY

I'M PICKY, INSENSITIVE, ARROGANT, EGOTISTICAL, CRANKY, CONNIVING, HOT-TEMPERED, WHINEY AND MEAN.

TO THANK YOU FOR ANOTHER YEAR OF PUTTING UP WITH MY INCESSANT YAMMERING, I'D LIKE TO TAKE YOU TO LUNCH!

WELL, NOW, **THERE'S** A TREAT.

WE BROUGHT DOUGHNUTS FOR SECRETARIES WEEK, CHARLENE, BUT SOMEONE TOOK BITES OUT OF ALL OF THEM BEFORE WE COULD BRING THEM TO YOU!
DONUTS
Secretaries Week

WE GOT YOU A CAKE, BUT THE WHOLE THING DISAPPEARED BY THE TIME WE ROUNDED UP ENOUGH NON-PLASTIC FORKS!
DONUTS
Secretaries Week

WE'D TOAST YOU WITH COFFEE, BUT SOMEONE DIDN'T TURN OFF THE POT LAST NIGHT AND THERE'S A HALF-INCH OF CRUD WELDED TO THE BOTTOM!
DONUTS
Secretaries Week

BESIDES, THE MUGS ARE ALL FILTHY BECAUSE SOMEONE DIDN'T TAKE HIS TURN AT KITCHEN DUTY!!!
NEVER LET IT BE SAID THIS OFFICE DOESN'T KNOW HOW TO PARTY.
Secretaries Week

BINKMAN NEEDED THIS ASAP!
I SENT A COPY FOR OVERNIGHT DELIVERY. HE'LL HAVE IT IN THE MORNING.

OVERNIGHT ?? WHAT IS THIS, THE STONE AGE ?!

WE HAVE A $5,000 ELECTRONIC TRANSMITTAL SYSTEM, AND YOU CAN'T GET IT WHERE IT NEEDS TO GO FASTER THAN OVERNIGHT ??!!

CALL ME A ROMANTIC... I STILL BELIEVE IN THE POWER OF THE PRINTED PAGE....
GUISEWITE

HEY, THERE... DON'T I KNOW YOU?
ME? NO. I DON'T THINK SO.

YOU LOOK SO FAMI-LIAR. HAVE YOU EVER BEEN ON TV?
TV?? NO. NO TV! NO! NEVER!

YES YOU HAVE...YOU'RE...YOU'RE... VIDEO-DATE #4327!! "LOVES HOLDING HANDS IN THE MOONLIGHT"!!!

HE SIGNED UP, TOO, OR HE WOULDN'T KNOW!
I HAVE A SINGLE NEPHEW IF YOU'RE REALLY THAT DESPERATE.

DOUGHNUTS!
CROISSANTS!
MUFFINS!
WAFFLES!
PANCAKES!
NO...
NOT YET...

PIZZA!
CANDY!
CHIPS!
CHEESEBURGERS!
FRIES!
BROWNIES!
CHOCOLATE!
SH!

PIE!
ICE CREAM!
MASHED POTATOES!
CUPCAKES!
GRAVY!
PUDDING!
QUIET!!
CLICK! CLICK! CLICK!

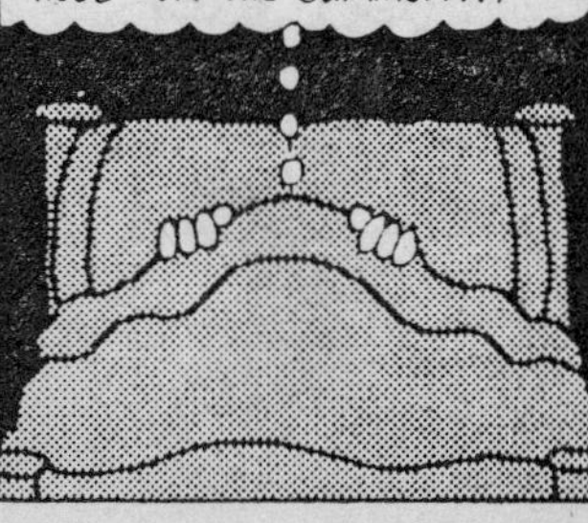
RIGHT ON SCHEDULE... FOUR WEEKS UNTIL SWIMSUIT SEASON, AND THE "SCREAMING CALORIES" HAVE MIGRATED TO TOWN AND MOVED INTO MY NEIGHBORHOOD FOR THE SUMMER...

WHEN I'M HUNGRY, I EAT.
WHEN I'M THIRSTY, I EAT.
WHEN I'M TIRED, I EAT.
WHEN I'M NERVOUS, I EAT.
WHEN I'M BORED, I EAT.
WHEN I'M ANNOYED, I EAT.
WHEN I'M HAPPY, I EAT.
WHEN I'M SAD, I EAT.

Diet Diary

IN YET ANOTHER IRONIC TWIST OF FATE, NOTHING GIVES A PERSON THE RESOLVE TO START WORKING OUT LIKE SPENDING THE DAY IN CLOTHES THAT ARE TOO TIGHT...
I HAVE TO WORK OUT... I HAVE TO WORK OUT...

...AND NOTHING TAKES THE RESOLVE AWAY LIKE GOING HOME AND CHANGING INTO WORKOUT CLOTHES...
HM! SO BAGGY! SO COMFY! I'M NOT THAT OUT OF SHAPE AFTER ALL!

OH, I KNOW, CATHY... WOMEN IN OUR FAMILY HAVE STRUGGLED WITH THE "THIGH PROBLEM" SINCE THE BEGINNING OF TIME...
S
P

LOSE HALF AN INCH...GAIN TWO INCHES...LOSE A QUARTER INCH...GAIN AN INCH AND A HALF... GENERATION AFTER GENERATION....
S
P

...AND IF YOU THINK IT'S HARD NOW, WAIT'LL YOU TURN 40! HOO, BOY!! GRANDMA WENT UP TWO PANT SIZES IN THREE WEEKS!!

...AND MOTHERS WONDER WHY WE QUIT TURNING TO THEM FOR PEP TALKS....

...NO, SEE, JENNA HAD BOBBY'S CHILD EVEN THOUGH HE MARRIED PAM, WHO MIGHT STILL BE DEAD, UNLIKE APRIL, WHO WAS DEFINITELY MURDERED WHILE J.R. WAS STUCK IN THE PSYCHO WARD BY HIS ILLEGITIMATE SON WHILE CLIFF WAS...OH, IRVING! THEY WERE MY FRIENDS! MY FRIDAY NIGHT FAMILY, AND NOW THEY'RE GONE FOREVER!

CATHY, IT WAS JUST A TV SHOW.
OH, I KNOW...sniff... THIS IS SO SILLY...
SURE YOU'RE OK?
OF COURSE. HA, HA! IT WAS JUST A SILLY, SILLY TV SHOW!

WE'LL NEVER KNOW WHAT CALLIE NAMED THE BABY!!!

WANT TO GO FOR A WALK, ELECTRA ??... WAKE UP!... WANT TO GO OUTSIDE ??
SNORE
POKE POKE

OH! YOU WANT TO GO FOR A DRIVE? WELL, OK... IT'S ALMOST MIDNIGHT, BUT I GUESS WE COULD GO FOR A DRIVE...

...NOW YOU WANT TO STOP AT THE STORE FOR SOME DOG BIS-CUITS? DO YOU THINK YOU REALLY NEED DOG BISCUITS??
SNORE

MY CAT HAD A CRAVING FOR NACHOS AND GUACAMOLE.
GET A LIFE...
Chips
Guisewite

THE COUCH IS WHERE DIETS DIE, ELECTRA! WE ARE NOT GOING NEAR THAT COUCH TONIGHT!!

CLICK

IF THE COUCH IS WHERE DIETS DIE, THE BED IS WHERE THEY GO TO GET BURIED....
CLICK
ICE CREAM
COOKIES

6:00PM: RACE OUT OF OFFICE. DRIVE AS FAST AS POSSIBLE TO GYM BEFORE ALL PARKING SPACES ARE GONE...

CIRCLE LOT 17 TIMES... PARK HALF A MILE AWAY... RUN TO GYM...

FLING SELF INTO WORKOUT CLOTHES BEFORE LINES FORM FOR ALL GOOD MACHINES...

PACE BETWEEN MACHINES... GIVE UP AND JOIN ADVANCED "STEP CLASS" HALF-WAY IN THE MIDDLE...

ZOOM HOME. WALK AND FEED DOG. SHOWER. WASH AND DRY HAIR. REDO CONTACTS. REDO MAKEUP. FIND, IRON AND PUT ON KICKY, CASUAL EVENING OUTFIT...

THUS CONCLUDES THE FIRST AND LAST DAY OF THE "AFTER-WORK WORKOUT" PROGRAM.

I COULDN'T GET THESE JEANS OVER MY HIPS LAST WEEK, AND NOW THEY'RE ZIPPED! I CAN LIVE AGAIN!! I CAN LOVE! I CAN FROLIC!!

...NO! NOT THOSE TWO POUNDS AGAIN! I ALREADY LOST THOSE TWO POUNDS!

WHAT ARE YOU DOING BACK AGAIN?? I'VE GOTTEN RID OF YOU TEN TIMES THIS YEAR!! CAN'T YOU TAKE A HINT??!

YOU ARE NOT WELCOME HERE ANYMORE! GO AWAY! FIND SOMEWHERE ELSE TO SPEND THE SUMMER AND TAKE ALL YOUR FAT LITTLE FRIENDS WITH YOU!!!

IF THE BODY IS A TEMPLE, WHY DOES MINE KEEP FEELING LIKE A MOTEL?
Guisewite

I DID IT! I BROUGHT UP THE "L" WORD!
YOU BROUGHT UP THE "L" WORD??

I ALWAYS THOUGHT IT WAS JUST SOMETHING THAT HAPPENED TO OTHER PEOPLE, BUT THEN I THOUGHT, WAIT A MINUTE....

I NEED IT! I DESERVE IT! I AM GOING FOR IT!!

I HAVE NO IDEA IF SHE'S DISCUSSING "LOVE" OR "LIPOSUCTION".
NOR DO I KNOW WHICH ONE WOULD MAKE ME MORE JEALOUS.

THAT DOES IT.

I DID NOT SUFFER ALL WEEK TO HAVE TO LISTEN TO A MACA-DAMIA NUT COOKIE SCREAMING AT ME DOWN THE HALL!

I KNOW YOU'RE IN HERE, YOU MISERABLE COOKIE! NOW SHUT UP AND LEAVE ME ALONE!!!
BAM BAM

.....HM! COOKIE CRUMBS! NO CALORIES!

FOOTBALL'S OVER...
BASKETBALL'S ALMOST OVER...
HOCKEY'S ALMOST OVER...
BASEBALL'S TOO NEW TO COUNT...

COME TO ME, IRVING! SAY THE WORDS I'VE WAITED THROUGH 243 PLAYOFF GAMES TO HEAR!!

IRVING, ON OUR FIRST DATE, I SPECIFICALLY ASKED IF YOU HAD ANY INTEREST IN GOLF.
HA, HA! WHO KNEW?!

YOU PROMISED ME YOU HATED GOLF! YOU SWORE THERE WERE NO "GOLF GENES" IN YOUR FAMILY!

I HAVE YEARS INVESTED IN THIS RELATIONSHIP! YOU CAN'T JUST WALTZ IN HERE AND ANNOUNCE THAT YOU'RE A GOLFER!!
I'M A GOLF-ER!!

WHY IS IT THE ONLY TIME MEN REALLY CHANGE IT'S INTO SOMETHING TOTALLY AGGRAVATING?
8

WHEN ARE YOU GOING TO GOLF? YOU WORK LATE EVERY NIGHT.
NOT ANYMORE!
YOU SPEND THE WEEK-END AT THE OFFICE.
NOT ANYMORE!
GOLF

IRVING, I'VE BEGGED YOU TO QUIT WORKING LATE AND ON THE WEEKENDS ALL YEAR!
AND YOU WERE RIGHT! I FEEL GREAT!
GOLF

YOU WERE SUPPOSED TO SPEND THE TIME WITH ME! WHAT ABOUT ME?! ME!! ME!!

YOU SHOULD GOLF, TOO! HONESTLY, CATHY, YOU NEED TO LEARN TO RELAX!
GOLF

...UNBELIEVABLE! I WAS ON A LONG PAR FOUR AND WAS ON IN THREE AND TWO-PUTTED!

...I HAD A GREAT TEE-SHOT ON A 185-YARD PAR THREE AND LEFT MYSELF WITH AN EIGHT-FOOT PUTT AND JUST MISSED GETTING MY FIRST BIRDIE!

I HIT MY SECOND SHOT ON THE 17TH HOLE, PUSHED IT INTO THE TRAP AND SUNK MY PUTT FOR A SANDY!!

WHY NON-GOLFING WOMEN WHO ARE INVOLVED WITH GOLFING MEN NO LONGER ASK, "HOW WAS YOUR DAY?"

GOLF!! IT'S ALL IRVING TALKS ABOUT! IT'S ALL HE THINKS ABOUT!!

HE'S AT THE DRIVING RANGE... ...ON THE PRACTICE PUTTING GREEN... HE'S BOOKING FOURSOMES TWO MONTHS AHEAD!

SO WHAT, CATHY? IT'S JUST A SPORT. JUST AN INNOCENT SPORT!

AT LEAST IF HE WERE WITH ANOTHER WOMAN I'D UNDERSTAND WHY HE WAS ENJOYING HIMSELF!!
Guisewite

IRVING TOOK UP GOLF, MOM!!
THERE, THERE... IT'S JUST A PHASE, CATHY.

I WON'T SEE HIM ALL SUMMER!
I KNOW... I THOUGHT THE SAME THING WHEN YOUR FATHER TOOK UP GOLF....

...AND IT WAS JUST A PHASE?
JUST A PHASE.

I'M GOING TO HIT A FEW BUCKETS OF BALLS, DEAR.
AACK! DAD!!
IT'S A LONG PHASE.

SWIMWEAR BUYER,
AGE 20-25:
THIS WOULD BE DARLING IF I LOST THREE POUNDS!

SWIMWEAR BUYER,
AGE 25-30:
THIS WOULD BE DARLING IF I LOST TEN POUNDS.

SWIMWEAR BUYER,
AGE 30 AND OVER:
THIS WOULD BE DARLING IF IT WERE WRAPPED LIKE A NOOSE AROUND THE SWIMWEAR DESIGNER'S SCRAWNY LITTLE NECK!!

MATURITY: LEARNING TO TURN ENERGY AWAY FROM OURSELVES AND ONTO OTHERS....
GUISEWITE

THE BIG NEWS IN SWIMWEAR THIS YEAR IS THE BUST!
I'M OUT OF HERE.
SWIMWEAR

NO! WAIT! SEE? THE SUITS HAVE BUILT-IN CUPS, PADDING AND FRILLS, ALL DESIGNED TO ADD A LITTLE MYSTERY TO WOMEN WHO ARE DROOPY, SAGGY OR TOTALLY FLAT!

IF EVERYONE KNOWS THESE ARE FOR WOMEN WHO ARE DROOPY, SAGGY OR FLAT, THERE IS NO MYSTERY!
CERTAINLY THERE'S MYSTERY.

THEY DON'T KNOW WHICH ONE OF THOSE YOU ARE, NOW, DO THEY??
I'M OUT OF HERE.

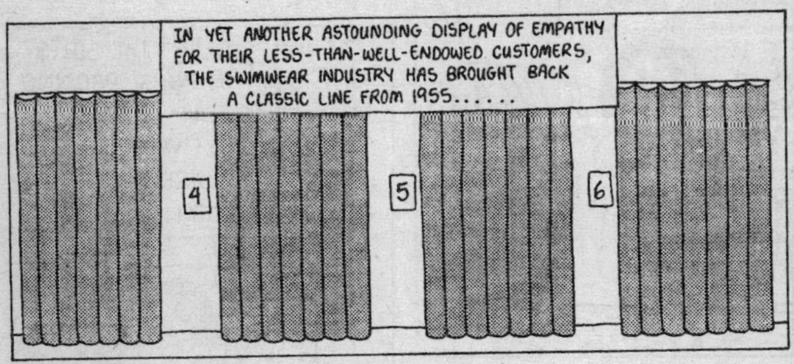
IN YET ANOTHER ASTOUNDING DISPLAY OF EMPATHY FOR THEIR LESS-THAN-WELL-ENDOWED CUSTOMERS, THE SWIMWEAR INDUSTRY HAS BROUGHT BACK A CLASSIC LINE FROM 1955......
4
5
6

"DON'T LIE ON YOUR STOMACH ON CEMENT."

THE LEGS ARE CUT TOO HIGH! THE COLOR IS NAUSEATING! THE "BUST" IS TWO INCHES ABOVE MY WAIST IF THE BACK'S PULLED DOWN FAR ENOUGH TO COVER MY REAR!

THE TRIPLE-REINFORCED, CRISS-CROSSED "TUMMY CONTROL PANEL" SQUASHES ME LIKE A SCREAMING GREEN SAUSAGE!!!

....AMAZING HOW THEY SETTLE DOWN WHEN YOU FIND A SUIT THAT COVERS THE MAIN FIGURE PROBLEM AREA.

YOU CAN HAVE RUFFLES ON THE TOP AND TRY TO LOOK AS THOUGH YOU DON'T HAVE A TEENY CHEST...

OR YOU CAN HAVE RUFFLES ON THE BOTTOM AND TRY TO LOOK AS THOUGH YOU DON'T HAVE A BIG REAR...

OR YOU CAN HAVE RUFFLES BOTH PLACES AND HOPE EVERY-ONE WILL GET THE RUFFLES CONFUSED AND START THINKING YOU'RE TRYING TO CONCEAL A CHEST THAT'S TOO BIG AND A REAR THAT'S TOO TEENY!
BINGO!

EXCELLENT CHOICE. WHY JUST FOOL THE MEN WHEN THERE'S A CHANCE WE CAN ALSO DELUDE OURSELVES?
GUISEWITE

BEACHWEAR EVOLUTION
1951: THE TWO-PIECE

1971: THE ONE-PIECE

1991: THE 36-PIECE
GLOVES! I NEED GLOVES! MY FINGERS MIGHT BE SHOWING!
SPF 36
SPF 25
SPF 42
SPF 15

OF THE 250,000 WORDS IN THE ENGLISH LANGUAGE, AND THE 25 ZILLION POSSIBLE COMBINATIONS, ALMOST NONE WILL HAVE THE IMPACT ON A WOMAN'S LIFE AS THIS ONE LITTLE OFF-HAND REMARK...

MARGO: ASKED FOR A NEW LOOK. GOT A NEW LOOK.
Salon

RUTH: ASKED FOR A NEW LOOK. GOT A NEW LOOK.
Salon

KIM: ASKED FOR A NEW LOOK. GOT A NEW LOOK.
Salon

CATHY: ASKED FOR A NEW LOOK. GOT A NEW LOOK.
Salon

CATHY'S AT HOME WITH A FAMILY EMERGENCY.
A FAMILY EMERGENCY?

IS SHE OK? ARE HER PARENTS OK??

CATHY! WHAT HAPPENED?? MR. PINKLEY SAID YOU HAD A FAMILY EMERGENCY!!

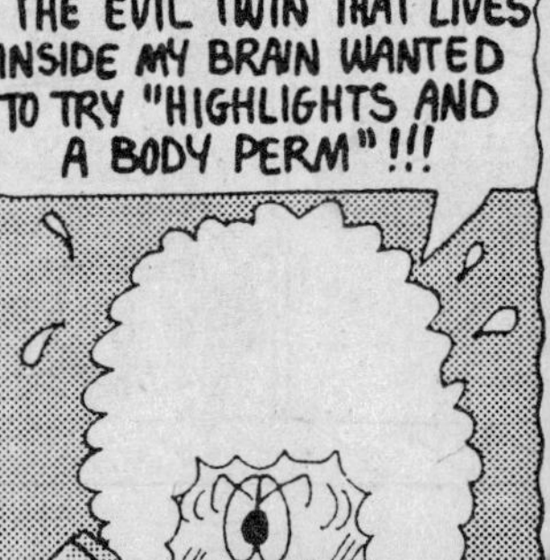
THE EVIL TWIN THAT LIVES INSIDE MY BRAIN WANTED TO TRY "HIGHLIGHTS AND A BODY PERM"!!!

...NO...TELL ME I DIDN'T HAVE ANYTHING DONE TO MY HAIR... IT WAS JUST A NIGHTMARE... IT **HAD** TO BE A NIGHTMARE...

WHEW! SORRY I'M LATE, CATHY! THERE WAS A JAM-UP ON THE 14TH HOLE AND...
YOU'RE NOT GOING TO SAY ANYTHING ABOUT MY HAIR?

YOUR HAIR?
MY HAIR!! MY HAIR IS RUINED! LOOK AT MY HAIR!

WHAT ABOUT YOUR HAIR?
IRVING, I USED TO HAVE LONG, STRAIGHT, BROWN HAIR AND NOW IT'S GROSS! IT'S REPULSIVE!!

IT LOOKS FINE TO ME.
THERE'S NOTHING WORSE THAN A MAN WHO'S OBLIVIOUS TO HOW HIDEOUS YOU LOOK....

I CAN'T TALK RIGHT NOW, MOM!
UH, OH. WHAT COLOR IS YOUR HAIR, CATHY?
MILK

WHAT MAKES YOU THINK THERE'S ANY-THING WRONG WITH MY HAIR?
I'M YOUR MOTHER. THAT SOUNDED LIKE THE "HAIR VOICE".

MOM!
YES! THERE IT IS! THE "HAIR VOICE" WITH A HINT OF THE "DIET VOICE" AND JUST A TOUCH OF THE "LOVE-LIFE VOICE"!

I AM NOT HAVING THIS CON-VERSATION!!
ANOTHER DAY OF MOTHERHOOD, ANOTHER USELESS SKILL PERFECTED...
MILK

OH, IRVING, I JUST FEEL SO UGLY...I FEEL SO STUPID...
WEAR A HAT.

WEAR A HAT??
WEAR A HAT. CALL THE SALON. MAKE THEM FIX YOUR HAIR. CRISIS OVER! WHAT'S THE BIG DEAL?

SLAM!

MEN: ALL SOLUTION, NO SYMPATHY.

WHY DIDN'T YOU TELL THE STYLIST YOU HATED YOUR HAIR?
SHE TOLD ME I LOOKED BEAUTIFUL AND SOME LITTLE PART OF ME WANTED TO BELIEVE HER.

OH, CATHY...
WELL, EXCUSE ME, BUT WHICH OF US IS NOT JUST A COMBINATION OF OTHER PEOPLE'S OPINIONS?...WHICH OF US IS NOT SO HUNGRY TO FEEL BEAUTIFUL TO SOMEONE THAT WE WILL BELIEVE IT EVEN FROM THE LIPS OF...

AAACK!!

I WANT TO SPEAK TO THE LUNATIC WHO RUINED MY LIFE!!
NOW, THAT'S BEAUTIFUL.

YOU DON'T LIKE YOUR HAIR?
I ASKED FOR HIGHLIGHTS AND A BODY PERM AND I GOT A PLATINUM BUBBLE!
Salon
Salon

I'VE SEEN FIFTY WOMEN ASK FOR HIGHLIGHTS AND A BODY PERM AND NONE OF THEM GOT PLATINUM BUBBLES!
Salon

I PAY THE SAME MONEY! I ASK FOR THE SAME THING! WHY DOES LIFE ALWAYS LOOK COMPLETELY DIFFERENT ON MY HEAD THAN ON EVERYONE ELSE'S ??!!
GENETICS.

MOTHER!
RUN FOR YOUR LIFE, DEAR. IT'S FOR YOU AGAIN.
Guisewite

...FUNNY HOW MUCH MORE WE'RE WILLING TO RISK AT THE END OF A RELATIONSHIP....

TA DA! MY HAIR! LOOK AT MY HAIR!
YOUR HAIR LOOKS LIKE IT ALWAYS LOOKS, CATHY.

YOU DIDN'T SEE ME LAST WEEK! MY HAIR WAS RUINED!!
IT DOESN'T LOOK ANY DIFFERENT TO ME.

THAT'S JUST IT! IT'S BACK TO NORMAL! IT COST $300, BUT IT LOOKS EXACTLY LIKE IT DID BEFORE I WENT IN FOR MY NEW LOOK!!! LIFE CAN BEGIN AGAIN!!

IT'S HARD TO EXPLAIN THE THRILL OF MAINTENANCE...

HI. REMEM-
BER ME?
AACK! NOT
YOU!!
EXICO
HAWAII
TRAVEL AGEN

YOU
PLANNED
A TRIP
FOR ME
A FEW
YEARS
AGO AND...
YOU CHANGED
DEPARTURE
DATES 12 TIMES...
CHANGED ITIN-
ERARIES SIX
TIMES...CALLED
ME 15 TIMES A
DAY FOR A MONTH
AND THEN CAN-
CELED THE TRIP!

GET OUT OF MY OFFICE!
GET AWAY FROM MY BRO-
CHURES! GO TORTURE SOME
OTHER TRAVEL AGENT!!
MEXICO

I'M NOT REALLY THE
"REPEAT-BUSINESS" TYPE.
TRAVEL
SLAM!
CLOS

VACATION PLANNING: THE MARRIED PERSON
ARE THE ROOMS CONFIRMED FOR EACH AND EVERY NIGHT? CAN I RESERVE SEAT SELECTIONS TWO MONTHS IN ADVANCE? WILL YOU PROVIDE COPIES OF OUR DAILY ITINERARY FOR ALL OUR RELATIVES AND BABY SITTERS?
TRAVEL AGENT

VACATION PLANNING: THE SINGLE PERSON
HOW MANY MINUTES BEFORE THE PLANE TAKES OFF CAN I CANCEL AND GET ALL MY MONEY BACK?
TRAVEL AGENT

HOW MANY WILL BE TRAVELING ?
TWO ... YES. DEFINITELY TWO.

TWO IS PERFECT. TWO OF US. "US." I LIKE THE SOUND OF THAT! TWO! YES! TWO OF US!

OUR TRIP. VERY ROMANTIC. JUST THE TWO OF US! A TWOSOME! A COUPLE!! YES!! A TRIP FOR TWO!

AND THE NAME OF YOUR TRAVEL-ING COMPANION?
LET'S JUST LEAVE THAT BLANK FOR A WHILE, OK?

I WANT THE CHEAPEST POSSIBLE RATE FOR TWO NIGHTS EACH AT SIX DIFFERENT QUAINT BED-AND-BREAKFASTS, WITH A ROOM IN EACH THAT OPENS ONTO A VERANDA OVERLOOKING THE SEA!
TRAVEL AGENT

HOW LOVELY! AND THIS IS FOR...?
THE FIRST WEEK OF JULY.

JULY?? JULY OF THIS YEAR??! HA, HA! THAT'S A GOOD ONE! HOO, HA!! JULY!! HA, HA, HA!!!

...WHEW! THANKS, I NEEDED THAT! SERIOUSLY, NOW, WHEN DID YOU WANT TO TRAVEL?
NEXT WEEK, AND DID I MENTION I'M USING BONUS MILES FOR THE AIRFARE?
TRAVEL AGENT

IF IRVING CAN'T GO ON VACATION WITH ME AND I GET DESPERATE, DO YOU WANT TO GO, CHARLENE?
YOU WANT ME FOR A "BACKUP"? I HARDLY THINK SO.

OH, COME ON... I'VE BEEN YOUR "BACK-UP DATE" ON A THOUSAND SATURDAY NIGHTS.
WOMEN DON'T DO THAT TO WOMEN ANYMORE.

YOU WERE DOING THAT TO ME TEN MINUTES BEFORE YOU MET SIMON!!
BUT NO MORE! IT'S OVER! SPINELESS WOMEN WHO DROP EVERYTHING FOR THE WHIMS OF MEN DON'T EXIST ANYMORE! THEY'RE GONE, CATHY! GONE FROM THE FACE OF THE EARTH!

EVEN WHEN IT'S A REALLY ICKY BREED, AT LEAST ONE OF US MOURNS ITS EXTINCTION.
COFFEE ROOM

JUST IMAGINE, IRVING... WE COULD SPEND TWO WEEKS EXPLORING THIS BEAUTIFUL LITTLE STRETCH OF CALIFORNIA...

LOOK... THERE ARE MOUNTAINS, BEACHES, DESERTS, ISLANDS, MUSEUMS, HISTORICAL SITES....
THE DESERT
MUSEUMS

CATHY, THIS IS THE ONLY CHANCE WE'LL HAVE TO GO AWAY TOGETHER ALL YEAR. ONLY ONE THING REALLY MATTERS....

742 GOLF COURSES WITHIN A 60-MILE RADIUS.
YES!!
GOLF

A COLORADO RAFT TRIP... THIS LOOKS GREAT!
I JUST SPENT A WEEK PLANNING A TRIP TO CALIFORNIA FOR YOU.
USA
COLORADO
UTAH
OHIO

....WAIT! HAWAII! MAYBE HAWAII IS BETTER!...OR MAINE! I FORGOT ABOUT MAINE!
MAINE

WHY DON'T I JUST WORK UP AN ITINERARY FOR EVERY STATE IN THE COUNTRY AND PREPARE A LITTLE SLIDE SHOW FOR YOU AND YOUR ALLEGED TRAVELING COMPANION TO MULL OVER ??!!
OH, NO. HA, HA! DON'T BE SILLY!

THAT WOULD BE EXCLUDING ALL OF EUROPE!!
EUR
FRANCE
ITALY

WE HAVE TO MAKE SOME DECISIONS ABOUT OUR VACA-TION TONIGHT, IRVING.
I HAVE TO WORK LATE TONIGHT. HOW ABOUT TOMORROW NIGHT?

CLIENT DINNER. HOW ABOUT LUNCH ON THURSDAY?
THURSDAY'S NO GOOD. HOW ABOUT LUNCH TODAY?
I CAN'T TODAY. LET'S TALK IN THE MORNING.
I HAVE A MEET-ING AT 9:00.
HOW ABOUT 10:00?
8:30.
8:45.

ODDS OF THIS COUPLE STARTING AND FINISHING A VACATION IN THE SAME TWO-WEEK PERIOD:
0
-5

MAYBE WE SHOULD GO TO NEW ORLEANS, CATHY.
NEW ORLEANS. PARTY CLOTHES. FLOWY BLUE SKIRT... SILK TOP... YELLOW DRESS....

OR MAYBE A DRIVE THROUGH ARIZONA.
ARIZONA. WESTERN LOOK. BEIGE PANTS, GREEN TANK TOP... NO. KHAKI SHORTS, TAN BLAZER... NO. IVORY JACKET, TAN CULOTTES...

HOW ABOUT A CRUISE?
CRUISEWEAR... PINK SUNDRESS... NO. BLACK COCKTAIL DRESS... NO. WHITE SUNDRESS, RED COCKTAIL DRESS... NO. DRESSY SWEATSUIT... NO...

WHAT DO YOU THINK?
I HAVE NO IDEA. MY ENTIRE BRAIN IS BEING USED UP BY MY CLOSET.

WE DECIDED ON THE NEW MEXICO TRIP AND WANT THE SPECIAL $150 FARE.
THE $150 FARE IS ONLY GOOD IF YOU'RE FLYING AT 10:00 PM ON A TUESDAY AND GIVE SIX WEEKS' ADVANCE NOTICE.

IF YOU BOOK FOUR WEEKS AHEAD AND TRAVEL IN AN EXCURSION OF SIX WITH ONE PERSON PAYING FULL FARE, YOU CAN GET THE $275 RATE...

FLY AT MIDNIGHT TO A CITY BEGINNING WITH THE LETTER "W", STAY OVER TWO THURSDAYS AND YOU MAY QUALIFY FOR THE $300 FARE...
THAT DOES IT! I'LL CALL THE AIRLINES MYSELF!

...WE'RE SORRY. ALL RESERVATION AGENTS HAVE LEFT THEIR POSTS TO GO TAKE AN ASPIRIN....
Guisewite

I FOUND TWO SEATS AT THE $350 RATE, BUT THE FARE EXPIRES AT MIDNIGHT.
TRAVEL AGENT

IRVING, YOU HAVE TO COMMIT! COMMIT NOW!! NO REFUNDS! NO CHANGES!! THE FARE EXPIRES AT MIDNIGHT! THE FARE EXPIRES AT MIDNIGHT!!

OUR RELATIONSHIP EXPIRED AT 4:15.
TRAVEL AGENT
GUISEWITE

OUR SINGLE DAUGHTER IS GOING AWAY WITH A SINGLE MAN.

THAT'S NICE.

OUR AGING UNMARRIED DAUGHTER IS TAKING OFF TO WHO-KNOWS-WHERE WITH WHAT'S-HIS-NAME.

UM HM.

I'M LOOKING FOR A BREEZY YET CHIC LONG SUMMER DRESS IN A MINT GREEN WRINKLE-RESISTANT FABRIC FOR MY VACATION NEXT WEEK!
NEW FALL ARRIVALS
FALL
FALL FASHION

...OKAY, IT COULD BE PANTS AND A JACKET, BUT SUMMERY! CHIC AND SUMMERY!
FALL
NEW FALL RRIVALS

...OKAY, IT COULD BE ANYTHING! ANYTHING FOR SUMMER! I HAVE TO HAVE SOME NEW SUMMERY THING FOR MY TRIP!!!

HOW ALL THE REALLY ICKY TANK TOPS FINALLY GET SOLD.
FALL FASHIONS
SUMME SALE
Guisewite

NOT TONIGHT, IRVING. I HAVE TO TRY ON ALL MY CLOTHES FOR OUR TRIP!

YOU HAVE TO TRY ON YOUR OWN CLOTHES??
OF COURSE! I HAVE TO TRY THEM ON SO I'LL KNOW WHAT TO BRING.

CATHY, THEY'RE **YOUR** CLOTHES! JUST STICK THEM IN A SUITCASE!!
STICK CLOTHES IN A SUITCASE WITHOUT TRYING THEM ON?!

WOMEN DON'T KNOW HOW TO PACK!
MEN DON'T HAVE TO GUESS WHAT SIZE THEY'LL BE BY THE TIME THE PLANE LANDS.
GUISEWITE

WHITE HEELS FOR THE WHITE DRESS... WHITE FLATS FOR THE WHITE SHORTS... WHITE TENNIS SHOES FOR THE BEACH...

TAN PUMPS FOR THE BEIGE DRESS... BONE FLATS FOR THE KHAKI PANTS... KHAKI WEDGIES FOR THE TAUPE SKIRT...

BEIGE SANDALS FOR THE BEIGE SHORTS... BEIGE MID-HEELS FOR THE BONE PANTS... BONE HIGH-HEELS FOR THE BONE DRESS...

1:30AM, AND WITH NO END IN SIGHT, THE PACKER IS ALREADY UP TO NINE PAIRS OF "NEUTRAL" SHOES.
GUISEWITE

CLOTHES, JEWELRY, UMBRELLA, SUNGLASSES, PAPER, ENVE-LOPES, PENS, STAMPS, TAPE, FIRST AID KIT, CONTACT STUFF, FLASHLIGHT, BOOKS TO READ, NEWSPAPERS TO GO THROUGH, LETTERS TO ANSWER, PROJECTS TO THINK ABOUT, BILLS TO PAY, SAFETY PINS, TOOTHPASTE, DEN-TAL FLOSS, LINTBRUSH, SCIS-SORS, STAPLER...

I FOUND ELECTRA SITTING IN MY SUITCASE. SHE WANTS TO COME ON MY VACATION.

WASN'T THAT SWEET? WASN'T THAT PRECIOUS?? ISN'T SHE THE MOST WONDERFUL THING YOU'VE EVER.....

...NICE TRY, MOTHER.

I'LL MISS YOU SO MUCH...
I'LL CALL YOU EVERY DAY...
GATE 87

I'LL THINK OF YOU EVERY SECOND, MY DARLING...

YOU'RE GOING TO CARRY ALL THAT ON?!!

WHY DO I GET THE FEELING THIS VACATION WOULD BE MORE ROMANTIC IF ONE OF US WEREN'T GOING ON THE TRIP?

CAN YOU BELIEVE THESE SUMMER-SAVER FARES?? OUR TICKETS WERE ONLY $198!
$198?? OURS WERE ONLY $165!

OURS WERE $150!
OURS WERE ONLY $132 AND THE KIDS ARE FLYING FOR FREE!

SHUT UP! JUST SHUT UP AND SIT DOWN!!

GET OUT THE VIDEO, DEAR! IT LOOKS LIKE THE COUPLE IN ROW 28 PAID COACH!

I'M NOT REALLY HUNGRY.
I KNOW, IRVING... THE AIR PRESSURE IN THE CABIN MAKES YOUR CELLS EXPAND, CAUSING YOU TO FEEL FAT AND FULL.

OF COURSE, YOU HAVEN'T REALLY GAINED WEIGHT, BUT BECAUSE YOU FEEL AS IF YOU DID, IT'S COMMON TO EAT TOO MUCH OUT OF FRUSTRATION, STARTING A CHAIN REACTION OF OVEREATING THAT GUARANTEES YOU'LL GAIN WEIGHT BY THE END OF THE VACATION!

WHY WOULD I EAT IF I WEREN'T HUNGRY ?
WHY DIDN'T I GO WITH A GIRL-FRIEND ??

SHE SHOPPED. SHE PACKED.
SHE SHOPPED. SHE PACKED.

SHE RE-SHOPPED, RE-PACKED...
RE-SHOPPED, RE-PACKED...
RE-SHOPPED, RE-PACKED...

...UNTIL FINALLY, EXHAUSTED AND READY TO RELAX WITH THE MAN SHE LOVES, SHE ARRIVES AT THE RESORT WITH ONLY ONE THING ON HER MIND...

IS THE GIFT STORE OPEN?
IT'S MID-NIGHT, MA'AM.
I GUESS THAT MEANS THE DRIVING RANGE IS OUT.
REGISTRAT

IT USED TO TAKE ME DAYS TO UNWIND ON VACATION, BUT NO MORE! I'M ALREADY STRESS-FREE, CATHY!
I WAS STRESS-FREE BEFORE THE PLANE LANDED!
Desert Café

I AM COMPLETELY RELAXED!
HAH! WELL, I AM TOTALLY RELAXED!
Desert Café

I'M MORE RELAXED THAN YOU ARE!!
I'M SO RELAXED I'M BARELY BREATHING!
HAH!
HAH!

THE PRINCE AND PRINCESS OF MELLOWNESS APPEAR TO BE READY TO ORDER.
Desert Café

"KICKY LINEN SHORTS AND JACKET ARE PERFECT FOR TRAVEL".... HAH!

THE MODEL IN THE MAGA-ZINE WASN'T ON HER KNEES ON THE BATHROOM FLOOR WITH A TRAVEL IRON!
8

THE MODEL DIDN'T MENTION HOW TO IRON A DOUBLE-BREASTED JACKET ON A TWO-FOOT BATHMAT WITHOUT THE MOTEL LOGO GETTING EMBOSSED INTO THE SLEEVE!! HAH! THE MODEL NEVER....

YOU'VE BEEN IN THERE FOR AN HOUR, CATHY. ARE YOU SICK??
IN A MANNER OF SPEAKING...
8

WHERE'S THE ADDRESS OF THE RESTAURANT?
DIDN'T YOU STICK IT ON THE LIST OF MUSEUMS?

HOW WAS I SUPPOSED TO STICK IT ON THE LIST OF MUSEUMS?
I DON'T KNOW. WITH STUFF. DIDN'T YOU SEE MY NOTE ON THE TABLE?

HOW WAS I SUPPOSED TO SEE A NOTE ON THE TABLE??
WHAT WAS I SUPPOSED TO DO, PIN IT ON MY SHIRT??

TWO VACATIONING BUSINESS-PEOPLE ON DAY THREE OF "POST-IT NOTE" WITHDRAWAL.

OH, COME ON, CATHY... DON'T SPEND AN HOUR PUTTING ON MAKEUP! IT'S YOUR VACATION! YOU DON'T NEED MAKEUP!
KNOCK KNOCK!

I DON'T EVEN LIKE MAKEUP! YOU LOOK BETTER WITHOUT MAKEUP!! PLEASE.... PLEASE....NO MAKEUP!!!
KNOCK KNOCK

I'LL GO TAKE A WALK WHILE YOU PUT ON YOUR MAKEUP.
GUISEWITE

WHAT DO YOU WANT TO DO TODAY, IRVING?
PLAY GOLF!
TOUR INFORMAT

DON'T BE SILLY! YOU CAN GOLF ANY TIME! WE'RE SURROUNDED BY SPECTACULAR SCENERY HERE... RIVERS... WATERFALLS... MOUNTAINS... CAVES... ANCIENT INDIAN ARTIFACTS....
INN

WHY WOULD YOU FLY ALL THIS WAY TO DO SOMETHING YOU COULD DO AT HOME??
LOBBY

OKAY, OKAY... WHAT DO YOU WANT TO DO, CATHY?
GO SHOPPING!
LOBBY

HERE'S YOUR BALL, IRVING! IT WAS OVER IN THE WEEDS!
AACK! YOU MOVED THE BALL! YOU'RE NOT ALLOWED TO MOVE THE BALL, CATHY!

WHO CARES? WE'RE THE ONLY ONES OUT HERE!
IT'S AGAINST THE RULES! YOU CAN'T BREAK THE RULES!!

YOU HATE RULES!
BUT THIS IS A SPORT! IT'S NO FUN WITHOUT RULES! IT'S POINTLESS UNLESS EVERYONE PLAYS BY THE EXACT SAME RULES!

TO DO AFTER VACATION: GET RELATIONSHIPS DECLARED A "SPORT" AND PRINT UP RULE BOOKS FOR ALL THE MEN.
Guisewite

WHAT A ROUND! DO YOU BE-
LIEVE THAT SIXTH HOLE, CATHY?!

NO. WHEW! WHEN YOUR HAND RESTED ON MY ARM FOR THAT EXTRA SECOND ON THE FAIRWAY, I FELT AS IF WE WERE LOCKED IN A PERFECT MOMENT IN TIME... ...AND THEN YOUR EYES SORT OF LOOKED AWAY AS IF IT WAS AL-MOST TOO POWERFUL AND, OH, IRVING, I JUST WANTED TO....

WHAT?? THAT ISN'T GOLF! WHAT ABOUT THE GOLF GAME?!
I HAVE NO RECOLLECTION OF ANY GOLF GAME BEING PLAYED.

...ON THE BRIGHT SIDE, SOMEWHERE BETWEEN US IS THE COMPLETE EXPERIENCE.

I GOT TO GOLF YESTERDAY AND YOU GOT TO SHOP TODAY! WE'RE EVEN!
WE PLAYED 36 HOLES OF GOLF YESTERDAY. YOU WERE ONLY IN THAT STORE FOR EIGHT MINUTES!!
INN
NIKES
INN
INN

WE'RE COMPLETELY EVEN!
TEN HOURS OF GOLF DOES NOT EQUAL EIGHT MINUTES OF SHOPPING!!
INN
INN
FRONT DESK

HAH!
HAH!
HAH!
...OH, HERE! I CAN TAKE THAT PICTURE OF YOU TWO NOW.

WHY THE VACATION PHOTOS OFTEN HAVE NOTHING TO DO WITH THE VACATION.

DON'T LEAVE THE DOOR OPEN. YOU'LL LET ALL THE COLD AIR OUT! DON'T THROW YOUR TOWELS AROUND. WHAT WILL THE CLEANING PEOPLE THINK?!

DON'T GO OUTSIDE WITHOUT SUNSCREEN! DON'T FORGET YOUR TOOTHBRUSH SO YOU CAN BRUSH AFTER LUNCH!

DON'T DRINK COFFEE ON AN EMPTY STOMACH! DON'T USE BUTTER. IT WILL GO RIGHT TO YOUR THIGHS!

Dear Mother,
I'd write you a post-card about my vacation, except you seem to be on it with me.

ONE-WEEK VACATION...
WITH HIM EVERY DAY...
A THOUSAND EVENTS...
NO ONE TO TELL...
GOLF
POSTCAR

NO WAY TO PROCESS IT...
NO PERSPECTIVE...
NO INTERPRETATIONS...
NO REHASHES...
NO COUNTERPOINT...
NO PEP TALKS.....
POST

AAACK!!

...CATHY ?
SORRY, IRVING. GIRLFRIEND WITHDRAWAL.
GOLF

MMM! THIS IS GREAT! I LOVE ICE CREAM!
ME TOO! I LOVE CHOCOLATE!

ME TOO! CHOCO-LATE'S THE BEST! LET'S HAVE MORE CHOCOLATE!
CHOCOLATE WITH CHOCOLATE SPRINKLES!

THIS IS PERFECT! GREAT IDEA! HA, HA, HA! WE'RE EXACTLY ALIKE!

WHEW! THAT WAS FUN! LET'S GO FOR A SWIM!
THE SIMILARI-TIES COME SCREECHING TO A HALT.

1ST DAY OF VACATION:
LEISURELY DRIVE.

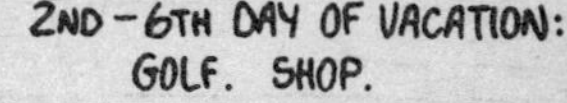

LAST DAY OF VACATION:
GOLF, SHOP, HORSEBACK RIDE, HIKE, FISH, SAIL, SWIM, READ, VOLLEYBALL, MOUNTAIN CLIMB, WATER SKI, HOT-AIR BALLOON, SNORKEL, TENNIS, TAKE PICTURES, TOUR MUSEUMS, TOUR GALLERIES, TOUR SITES, WRITE POSTCARDS, WRITE POSTCARDS, WRITE POSTCARDS

TRAINED BY YEARS IN BUSINESS, ANOTHER COUPLE HAS AN INVOLUNTARY RESPONSE TO A DEADLINE.

IT'S SO NICE HERE, CATHY. MAYBE WE SHOULD STAY AN EXTRA DAY.
WE CAN'T, IRVING! THE PLANE FARE WILL GO UP!

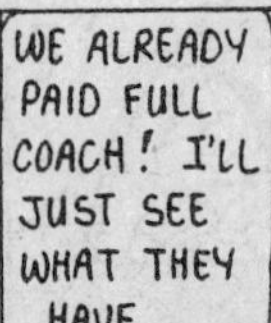

WE ALREADY PAID FULL COACH! I'LL JUST SEE WHAT THEY HAVE.
NO! DON'T CALL ATTENTION TO YOURSELF! THEY'LL LOOK UP YOUR RATE AND CHANGE IT!

THEY CAN'T CHANGE A FULL-FARE RATE!
PARDON THE RING! WRONG NUMBER! WE WEREN'T THINKING OF CHANGING ANYTHING! NO CHANGES!!

THEN AGAIN, WE'VE PROBABLY SPENT ENOUGH TIME TOGETHER...
WHAT IF THEY RECOGNIZED MY VOICE, BROUGHT UP OUR RECORD AND DUMPED IT???

WE'RE LATE! WE'RE LATE!
THE SUITCASE WON'T CLOSE! THE SUITCASE WON'T CLOSE!
INN
INN

WHERE'S THE SHUTTLE BUS?? WHERE'S THE SHUTTLE BUS??
RENTAL CAR RETURN

HURRY HURRY HURRY HURRY
GATES 150-156

NICE VACA-TION?
WHAT VACA-TION?!
DUE TO HEAVY TRAF-FIC, WE'LL BE SITTING ON THE RUNWAY FOR THE NEXT TWO HOURS.
INN
INN

WAS ELECTRA ANY TROUBLE WHILE I WAS ON VACATION, MOM?
GOODNESS, NO! WE BUILT A LITTLE THRONE FOR HER SO SHE COULD WATCH TV MORE COMFORTABLY!

I BROUGHT HER BOWLS OF FRESHLY COOKED CHICKEN AND RICE THREE TIMES A DAY... YOUR FATHER TOOK HER TO THE PARK FOUR TIMES A DAY...

...AND WE TOOK TURNS BRUSHING HER BEFORE WHEELING IN HER TOY SELECTION EACH MORNING.

ELECTRA! AREN'T YOU HAPPY TO SEE ME??
YEAH, RIGHT...
ELECTRA
ELECTRA
ELECTRA
ELECTRA

YOU'RE BACK, CATHY! OH, THANK HEAVENS! YOU'RE BACK!
WHY? DID SOMETHING HAPPEN WHILE I WAS GONE?
CHARLENE

ARE YOU KIDDING?! I HAD TO GO THROUGH THE WHOLE JULIA ROBERTS FIASCO WITH-OUT YOU!! THEN DONALD DUMPED MARLA...THEN DON-ALD PROPOSED TO MARLA...

PRINCE CHARLES DIDN'T SHOW FOR DI'S 30TH BIRTHDAY...ROSEANNE BARR REMARRIED HER HUSBAND... PRINCESS CAROLINE WAS SPOTTED WITH VINCENT LONDON... MERYL STREEP HAD ANOTHER BABY GIRL AND ONE OF THE KENNEDYS HAD A TATTOO REMOVED!!

DID ANYTHING HAPPEN THAT HAD ANYTHING TO DO WITH THE OFFICE?
NOT THAT I'M AWARE OF.

I HANDLED THE WEISS CRISIS JUST THE WAY YOU WOULD HAVE, CATHY!
WHEW, THANKS! I WOULD HAVE HATED TO FACE THAT ONE AGAIN AFTER MY VACATION!

FIRST I PUT IT IN MY "TO CALL" PILE... THEN I MOVED IT TO MY "TO WRITE TO" PILE... THEN I PUT IT BACK IN MY "TO CALL" PILE...

THEN I BURIED IT IN MY "TO READ" PILE, WHERE IT WAS ACCIDENTALLY PICKED OUT AND ROUTED TO BRIAN, WHO LOST IT FOR TWO DAYS AND JUST RETURNED IT THIS MORNING!

THE MENTOR PROGRAM BACKFIRES ONCE AGAIN.

I WENT ON VACATION. IT TOOK $900 AND TEN DAYS TO FORGET MY WORRIES.

I CAME HOME. IT TOOK NO MONEY AND 45 SECONDS TO FORGET MY VACATION.

SEE? YOU'RE ALREADY MORE EFFICIENT!

CAN YOU BELIEVE HOW MUCH THERE IS TO DO AFTER A VACATION, IRVING ??
WHAT DO YOU MEAN, CATHY ?

ARE YOU KIDDING ?? I HAVE TO WASH ALL THE CLOTHES I TOOK... IRON ALL THE CLOTHES I DIDN'T TAKE... PUT AWAY TEN PILES OF STUFF I MIGHT HAVE TAKEN...CLEAN THE WHOLE HOUSE... AND DO A MAJOR GROCERY RUN SO I'LL HAVE SOMETHING TO EAT THIS WEEK !!

I SENT MY CLOTHES TO THE CLEANERS, CALLED A MAID AND ORDERED A PIZZA.

MEN DON'T KNOW HOW TO MAKE THE HOLIDAY LAST.

I GAINED FIVE POUNDS ON MY VACATION! I CAN'T LET IRVING SEE ME THIS WAY!
CATHY, HE WAS WITH YOU ON VACATION! HE'S ALREADY SEEN YOU THAT WAY!

BUT HE HASN'T SEEN ME SINCE I FOUND OUT I GAINED IT!
HE WAS WITH YOU! HE WATCHED YOU GAIN IT!
BUT I LOOKED THINNER WHEN I DIDN'T KNOW I'D GAINED IT! I LOOK COMPLETELY DIFFERENT NOW!

READY FOR LUNCH, CATHY?
AACK!!

WHAT HAPPENED TO HER??
SEE? WHAT DID I TELL YOU?

OH, PLEASE, ELECTRA... DON'T BE MAD AT ME! HERE... LET'S PLAY WITH YOUR TOYS! LET'S BRUSH YOUR HAIR! LET'S HAVE SOME SNACKS!
DOG SNACKS

...UNBELIEVABLE. LOOK HOW MUCH HARDER I TRY WHEN YOU'RE ALOOF! WE ALL TRY HARDER TO PLEASE WHEN THE OTHER ONE'S ALOOF!

EH, I DON'T REALLY FEEL LIKE DINNER TONIGHT, IRVING.
GREAT! I'LL GO TO THE DRIVING RANGE!

CAN I HELP IT IF DOGS ARE BETTER AT HUMAN NATURE THAN HUMANS ARE?
GUISEWITE

NO MATTER HOW MUCH I'VE DONE, ANDREA'S DONE MORE AND ANDREA'S DONE IT BETTER.
LADIES

SHE'S THINNER, PRETTIER, MORE SUCCESSFUL... CONFIDENT, ARTICULATE, ORGANIZED, POLITICALLY INVOLVED, GLOBALLY ACTIVE... A PERFECT MARRIAGE PARTNER AND A BRILLIANT MOTHER!

SHE MAKES ME CRAZY! SHE MAKES ME SICK! SHE MAKES ME FEEL MY LIFE IS AT A PATHETIC STANDSTILL!!

WHY ARE YOU HAVING LUNCH WITH HER?
I WOULDN'T WANT HER TO THINK I DON'T LIKE HER.

ANDREA! YOU GOT YOUR HAIR CUT!
YES! HA, HA! I JUST MARCHED IN AND HAD IT ALL CHOPPED OFF, CATHY!

I HAVE SO MANY BETTER USES FOR MY TIME THAN MY HAIR!
AHEM... ME TOO!

I NEVER EVEN THINK ABOUT IT ANYMORE!
ME EITHER! HA, HA! WHO CARES ABOUT HAIR?!
Menu
Menu

FLUSHED WITH CONFIDENCE, SHE INSTANTLY COMPUTES HOW LONG SHE HAS UNTIL WHAT-SHE-DOESN'T-CARE-ABOUT STARTS BOINKING OUT IN LITTLE RINGLETS.
Menu

WE HAVEN'T HAD A DECENT CONVERSATION SINCE ZENITH WAS BORN, CATHY.
I KNOW, ANDREA.

ZENITH THIS... ZENITH THAT... I MUST HAVE MADE YOU CRAZY!
IT'S OK.

BUT I'M HERE NOW! ZENITH'S IN PRE-SCHOOL AND I CAN FINALLY TALK ABOUT SOMETHING BESIDES BEING HER MOMMY!
WEL-COME BACK! HOW ARE YOU?

WE'RE EXPECTING ANOTHER BABY!!

TA DA! HERE HE IS! HIS NAME IS GUS!
GUS??

WE JUST GOT THE AMNIO RESULTS, SO WE KNOW HE'S A HEALTHY BABY BOY, DON'T WE, GUS?

OH, CATHY... ZENITH IS IN PRE-SCHOOL FOR GIFTED 2-YEAR-OLDS... LUKE RESTRUCTURED HIS BUSINESS SO HE CAN STUDY FRENCH WITH HER IN THE AFTER-NOONS... I'M DOING SALES FROM MY COMPUTER AT HOME, AND NOW WE'RE EXPECTING AN IN-CREDIBLE LITTLE BABY BOY!!

WHAT'S NEW WITH YOU?

OF COURSE WE'RE RE-DOING OUR HOME IN KNOTTY COUNTRY PINE WITH HEIRLOOM QUILTS AND RUSTIC HAND-THROWN POTS FILLED WITH AZALEAS SNIPPED FROM MOMMY'S ORGANIC GARDEN WITH HER STAINLESS STEEL SMITH AND HAWKEN GARDENING SHEARS, GROWN IN THE RICH SOIL FROM DADDY'S SHARPER IMAGE COMPOST MAKER!

I ASKED FOR AN EX-TRA NAPKIN 10 MINUTES AGO!
IT'S RIGHT THERE.
DON'T TAKE IT PERSON-ALLY.

SHE'S STARTING HER FIFTH MONTH OF PREGNANCY, AND HER BER-SERK HORMONES ARE CAUSING HER TO BE MOODY, FORGETFUL AND CONGESTED.

SHE'S TOO BIG FOR REGULAR CLOTHES, BUT TOO SMALL FOR MATERNITY CLOTHES, MAKING HER FEEL SUSPENDED IN A SUR-REAL BLOATED SPACE WITH NOTH-ING TO REALLY "SHOW" FOR IT.

HOW MANY CHILDREN HAVE YOU HAD?
NONE OF MY OWN BUT 23 OF MY GIRLFRIENDS'.

I KNOW YOU HAVE TO GET BACK TO THE OFFICE, CATHY, BUT WOMEN DON'T GET ENOUGH CHANCES TO STOP AND SEE THAT IT'S ALL REALLY POSSIBLE.

A BRILLIANT 30-MONTH-OLD DAUGHTER... A SON ON THE WAY... A NURTURING HUSBAND... ...A BUSINESS I CAN RUN FROM MY HOME....

I'VE DONE IT, CATHY! I HAVE IT ALL!!

...AND IT'S ALL SCREAMING, BROKEN OR FILTHY.

LUKE! WHAT ARE YOU DOING HERE? ZENITH WAS SUPPOSED TO BE AT HER PRESCHOOL YOUNG PEOPLE'S CONCERT UNTIL 2:00!

BY 11:15, ZENITH HAD TAKEN OFF ALL HER CLOTHES, BITTEN THE CONDUCTOR IN THE KNEE AND GOADED THE KLEIN TWINS INTO A SHRIEKING CONTEST.

COMING THIS SOON AFTER THE POTTERY WORKSHOP INCIDENT, HER TEACHER SAID SHE HAD NO CHOICE BUT TO, QUOTE, "EXPEL THIS LITTLE L-U-N-A-T-I-C!"

LUNATIC!
SHE'S TOO ADVANCED FOR THAT CROWD, ANYWAY.
SHE ISN'T POTTY-TRAINED YET, DEAR.

ZENITH BAD!
OH, NO, HONEY! YOU CAUSED A LITTLE RIOT AT PRESCHOOL BUT YOU AREN'T BAD!

MAYBE MOMMY HASN'T SPENT ENOUGH TIME WITH YOU... MAYBE MOMMY'S SPENT TOO MUCH TIME WITH YOU... MAYBE MOMMY'S SPENT THE RIGHT AMOUNT OF TIME BUT DID EVERYTHING WRONG!

MOMMY BAD.
MOMMY BAD?!!

NICE TO SEE YOU'RE GETTING THE MOTHER-DAUGHTER THING OFF TO A HEALTHY START, ANDREA.

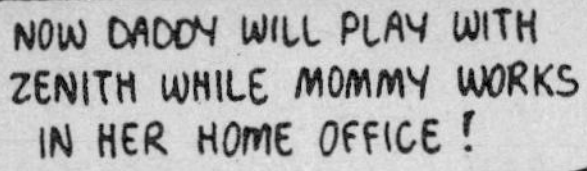
NOW DADDY WILL PLAY WITH ZENITH WHILE MOMMY WORKS IN HER HOME OFFICE!

DADDY'S BEEN OUT OF HIS OFFICE FOR TWO HOURS! MOMMY WAS SUPPOSED TO DO HER WORK IN THE MORNING!
MOMMY SPENT THE MORNING SCRAPING PLAY-DOH OUT OF HER COMPUTER KEYBOARD!

IT ISN'T DADDY'S FAULT THAT MOMMY IS DISOR-GANIZED!
DADDY HASN'T TRIED TO CONDUCT BUSINESS WITH A TWO-AND-A-HALF-YEAR-OLD HANG-ING FROM HIS NECK!!

ANOTHER COUPLE CROSSES THE FINE LINE BETWEEN CARE-GIVING AND GUILT-GIVING.

WE HAVE A GIFTED 30-MONTH-OLD DAUGHTER WHO'S IN NEED OF A NEW DAY-CARE ARRANGEMENT, AND WE'D LIKE TO TOUR YOUR FACILITY.
YOU MUST BE JOKING.

WE'D PREFER A MORE EDUCATIONAL ENVIRONMENT, BUT MIGHT CONSIDER ONE WHERE SHE COULD SIMPLY HONE HER SOCIAL SKILLS.
OUR NEXT OPENING IS IN 1998.

PLEASE! TAKE HER! JUST TWO CRUMMY HOURS A DAY! ANYTHING! TAKE HER!

HOW'D YOU DO?
ZENITH IS OUT OF THE QUESTION, BUT OUR UNBORN SON CAN GO TO DAY CARE WHEN HE'S SEVEN.

IF I DON'T WORK, WE CAN'T PAY ALL OUR BILLS... IF I DO WORK, IT TAKES MOST OF WHAT I MAKE TO PAY FOR DAY CARE.

IF I DON'T WORK, I GET CLAUSTROPHOBIC AND CRANKY. IF I DO WORK, I FEEL LIKE I'M DESERTING HER.

MOMMY'S ON THE GUILT-TRACK.

WE PLAYED MOZART TO ZENITH BEFORE SHE WAS BORN TO GIVE HER A FOUNDATION IN MUSIC... ...WE HUNG POSTCARDS FROM THE LOUVRE OVER HER CRIB TO ACQUAINT HER WITH THE ARTS...

WE'VE STUDIED EVERY BOOK ON THE EMOTIONAL AND INTELLECTUAL DEVELOPMENT OF A CHILD...

WE ARE **NOT** GOING TO HAND THIS LITTLE TREASURE OVER TO JUST **ANYONE** TO TAKE CARE OF!

ENGLISH! I MIGHT HAVE FOUND ONE WHO SORT OF SPEAKS ENGLISH!
HOW MUCH?

WELL, THAT'S THAT. IF A NANNY IS AVAILABLE, THERE'S ALWAYS SOME HIDEOUS REASON WHY.
SLAM!

IN THIS DAY AND AGE, IF SOMEONE'S STILL ON THE MARKET, THERE'S SOME HIDEOUS REASON WHY.

ANYTIME SOMEONE'S STILL OUT THERE LOOKING, THERE'S SOME HIDEOUS REASON WHY, AND THE EXACT SAME LAME EXCUSE!

MAYBE I JUST HAVEN'T FOUND THE RIGHT SITU-ATION YET!!
BINGO! HONESTLY, I'D ALMOST THINK YOU'D BEEN THROUGH THIS ONE YOUR-SELF, CATHY!

A FRIEND OF A FRIEND HEARD A RUMOR ABOUT THIS NEW HOME-CARE CENTER CALLED "GRANNY NANNIES". HELP ME ASK THE RIGHT QUESTIONS, CATHY!

ARE THEY LICENSED?
ARE THEY EDUCATED?
HOW DO THEY DISCIPLINE?
HOW MANY CHILDREN PER ADULT?
WHAT ARE THEIR REFERENCES?
IS IT SAFE? IS IT CLEAN?
IS IT A WHOLESOME, HEALTHY, HAPPY, CREATIVE ENVIRONMENT?

AACK! THAT'S MY MOTHER!
Granny Nannies
Granny Nannies

WOULD MY DAUGHTER TURN OUT ANYTHING LIKE HER??
Granny Nannies

I DIDN'T KNOW YOU WERE STARTING "GRANNY NANNIES," MOM!
NEITHER DID I, CATHY.
Granny Nannies

I WHISPERED THE IDEA AS A LITTLE JOKE TO FLO IN THE LADIES ROOM AT THE MALL.
Granny Nannies
Granny Nannies

...BY 6:00 THAT EVENING WE HAD 2,400 APPLICATIONS, 150 BRIBE OFFERS AND 49 PARENTS STANDING ON THE PORCH CLUTCHING VIDEOS OF THEIR ADORABLE CHILDREN.
Granny

IF NECESSITY IS THE MOTHER OF INVENTION, DESPERATION IS THE GRANDMA.
Guisewite

YOU SET UP THIS WHOLE DAY-CARE CENTER IN A WEEK??
OH, NO, CATHY. UNLIKE YOUR MOTHER, I HAVE SEVEN ADORABLE GRANDCHILDREN OF MY OWN!

I ALWAYS KEEP THIS ROOM FILLED WITH TOYS FOR WHEN THEY COME TO VISIT.
Granny Nannies

...SEE? THERE'S THEIR LITTLE MUSIC CORNER... THEIR READ-ING CORNER... AND HERE'S A WALL DEVOTED TO THEIR DAR-LING LITTLE ART PROJECTS!
Granny Nannies

SORRY, MOM.
PEER PRESSURE NEVER GOES AWAY. IT JUST TAKES UP MORE SQUARE FOOTAGE.
Granny Nannies

PLEASE! PLEASE! PLEASE!
WHINING WILL GET YOU NOWHERE, YOUNG LADY!
Granny Nannies

PLEASE!
WE'RE NOT DISCUSSING IT UNTIL YOU CHANGE THAT TONE OF VOICE!
Granny Nannies

PLEASE!! BUMP ONE OF THOSE OTHER KIDS AND PUT MY DAUGHTER ON YOUR DAY-CARE LIST!!
Granny Nannies
SIGN UP

FLO'S VERY GOOD WITH CHILDREN.
THESE BIG ONES ARE TOUGH, THOUGH.
THPT!
Granny Nannies
SIGN UP

I TRIED CALLING YOU EARLIER, CATHY.
I WENT TO SEE ANDREA. YOU ALWAYS GOLF ON MONDAY.

I DON'T ALWAYS GOLF ON MONDAY.
YOU ALWAYS SAY YOU DON'T, BUT YOU ALWAYS DO, IRVING.

I DON'T ALWAYS DO ANY-THING!
AND YOU ALWAYS GO CRAZY WHEN I SAY YOU ALWAYS DO SOMETHING! YOU'VE ALWAYS HAD A PROBLEM WITH THE CONCEPT OF ALWAYS!

AAUGH!!
WHAT WOMAN CAN RESIST USING THE ONE REAL PIECE OF KNOWLEDGE WE HAVE ABOUT THEM?

HOW WAS YOUR VISIT WITH ANDREA, CATHY?
IN A WORLD OF FINANCIAL RUIN, I STILL HAVE A DECENT JOB, CHARLENE.

IN A WORLD OF CRUMBLING RELATIONSHIPS, I'M STILL SPEAKING TO SOMEONE I USUALLY CARE ABOUT.

IN A WORLD OF MORAL CHAOS, I HAVE A PROUD, HAPPY AND RE-WARDING LIFE!!
SHE'S PREGNANT AGAIN, ISN'T SHE?

OUCH.
FUNNY HOW HARD THEY CAN KICK WHEN THEY'RE THAT LITTLE.

I LOVE ANDREA FOR BEING PREGNANT AGAIN, AND I HATE HER FOR IT, CHARLENE.
LOVE AND HATE ARE FIRST COUSINS, CATHY.

I WANT WHAT SHE HAS... I WANT MORE THAN SHE HAS!
JEALOUSY AND GREED ARE BROTHER AND SISTER.

PART OF ME WORRIES THAT I COULDN'T HANDLE IT AS WELL AS SHE DOES... ...BUT PART OF ME KNOWS I'D BE BETTER!
WELL, HELLO, "UNCLE INSECURITY" AND "AUNT CONFIDENCE"!

CATHY WILL BE A FEW MOMENTS. SHE'S HAVING A FAMILY REUNION IN THE LADIES ROOM.

WHAT ARE YOU WEARING TO ENTICE IRVING TO-NIGHT, CATHY?
I'M THROUGH WITH THE HOCUS-POCUS, CHARLENE.

NO MORE TRYING TO MANIPU-LATE HUMAN EMOTIONS WITH SOME RIDICULOUS COSTUME.

I AM CLAIMING RESPONSIBILITY FOR MYSELF! I ALONE AM IN CHARGE OF EVERYTHING THAT HAPPENS TO ME!!

WHAT'S THE COSMOPOLITAN MAGAZINE DOING IN YOUR BRIEF-CASE?
IT JUMPED OFF THE RACK AT THE SUPER-MARKET AND THREW ITSELF INTO MY CART.

IRVING, IT'S 9:00! WE WERE SUPPOSED TO GO OUT TO DINNER!
I TOLD YOU I WAS STOPPING AT THE DRIVING RANGE FIRST.

THAT WAS AT 5:00!
IT WAS UNBELIEVABLE! I WAS HITTING THEM STRAIGHT, ABOUT 185 YARDS, CATHY!!

YOU DID THAT FOR FOUR HOURS?!
YES! AND I OWE IT ALL TO THIS BEAUTY, THE MOST FORGIVING WOOD IN MY BAG!!

I HAVE MET HIS MISTRESS, AND SHE WEARS A LITTLE SOCK ON HER HEAD.

IRVING AND I STARTED LAST NIGHT WITH A HORRIBLE FIGHT AND WOUND UP HAVING ONE OF THE BEST EVENINGS OF OUR LIVES, CHARLENE!

CLASSIC! FACED WITH THE SHOCK OF IMPENDING BREAK-UP, YOU CLUNG TO EACH OTHER WITH A NEW PASSION.

IT DOESN'T MEAN YOU RESOLVED ANYTHING... JUST THAT YOU GAVE EACH OTHER A LITTLE VACA-TION FROM EXPERIENCING IT! YOU'LL BE AT EACH OTHER'S THROATS AGAIN WITHIN DAYS!

IF YOU'RE GOING TO HAVE LUNCH WITH A GIRLFRIEND, DON'T DO IT IMMEDIATELY FOLLOWING HER THERAPY APPOINTMENT.

THE MORTGAGE BILL: DULL NAUSEA. DON'T WANT TO LOOK. DON'T WANT TO THINK ABOUT IT.

THE GAS BILL: TOTAL FUTILITY. THE PHONE BILL: NUMBING. INCOMPREHENSIBLE. NO FEELING WHATSOEVER.

...AACK! WHAT IS **THIS**??!
THIS IS AN **OUTRAGE**!!
THIS IS AN **OFFENSE**!!
I AM NOT GOING TO STAND FOR THIS!!!

FEW THINGS CAN MAKE US COME ALIVE LIKE A CHRISTMAS CATALOG IN AUGUST.